Shared Purpose:

A Thousand Business Ecosystems, a Worldwide Connected Community, and the Future

James F. Moore
May 2013

Contents

Introduction: Business ecosystems and shared purpose

Business ecosystems are pretty simple: The goal is to get a lot of people to bring their creativity together and accomplish something more important than they can do on their own. In general, a business ecosystem tries to be wildly inclusive, and in its extreme tries to catalyze the productivity of a swarm. Apple and Google's app-making communities are obvious examples. Arab Spring was a swarm that helped oust entrenched dictators.

Business ecosystems almost guarantee disruptive results, because by breaking up a previously integrated design they reduce barriers to entry to new players, and encourage new people with new ideas, new money, new tools and new technologies to participate and create. In recent years the tech industry has become adept at using a variety of styles of business ecosystems, from heavily-funded, capital-intensive ecosystems such as Intel's that thirty years ago began to disrupt the integrated computing world, to today's community-driven and crowd sourced initiatives like Kickstarter and Quirky.

Now what do I mean by "shared purpose"? It's when people choose to work together to realize particular ideals and values. Or said another way, when people stop treating their economic life as "value free."

Nobel-prize-winning economist Oliver Williamson writes that 100 years ago the profession of economics split along two lines: one group went toward a price model, the other toward achieving shared purpose in organizations.[1] The price mechanism had the great advantage of making our economy more friction-free because you and I can trade freely even if you and I don't agree about values and purpose.

The combined effect of trillions of trades has shaped our society. And like the price mechanism for individuals, the unmanaged world market made conversations about values and shared purpose unnecessary. In the early 20th century this freed economies from the meddling of princes, from the whims of dictators, and from the oppressions of totalitarianism. It seemed a brilliant advance, a fundamental technology on par with steam, electric lights and telephones, medical specialties, cars and roads.

1

I look at our economic system as a technology, or more precisely as a combination of technologies. All technologies eventually "run out of steam"—an apt metaphor. All beneficial technologies follow an S-curve of effectiveness. They take some time to get going, take off and in the best cases transform society, and then reach a point of diminishing value. We invented a nearly value-free economic mechanism. The application of this technology in combination with others brought remarkable progress for many. Now in the 21st century our global situation has changed dramatically. We have different problems, we have modern science and engineering, and we are in global communication with each other. Yet, we are now up against the limits of our current economic technology.

As we entered the latter half of the 20th century our economic machine began to creak and grown. As a short-cut, it had left out of its accounts so-called "externalities": the environment; the poor and others outside of the mainstream economy; as well as health degradation—obesity, heart disease, depression, diabetes and inflammation-driven diseases—even among those in the most affluent; and social unrest among those closed out, expressed in terrorism, rioting and small-scale but widespread resource wars. Our apparatus for shared action, for achieving shared purpose, is broken or non-existent.

In the pages that follow I will describe, working as a kind of business anthropologist, a new form of organization, a vast-internetworked collection of business ecosystems that shows promise in achieving shared purposes, sharing value among many contributors, and in bringing the benefits of technology to a range of people, cultures and problems far beyond what earlier systems have achieved. It was created by people with values and shared purposes interacting with each other and evolution over many years. Like most things that have evolved, it is more complex and more counter-intuitive and far more effective than anything a person could make up.

We need to have a larger conversation about the future. My contribution is to share the inner workings of a particular ecosystem approach that not only is disrupting large swaths of the tech industry, but may have the potential to mobilize talent to solve other big problems.

To start the conversation consider three phases of recent technology industry leadership:

- First generation business ecosystems led by monopoly or near-monopoly leaders;

2

- Second generation business ecosystems generated mostly by volunteers: open source, gift economy, DIY, and peer production communities pursuing well-considered ideals and values;

- Third generation business ecosystems that are a hybrid of the first two.

One of the third generation's peculiar characteristics is that these ecosystems themselves form communities. At the base is a connected community that is an informal society of individuals and companies who share common purposes. These purposes include shared technology and standards, as well as business practices such as encouraging differentiation and cooperation to help all members succeed. Thriving on the base are many business ecosystems. We will examine these third generation business ecosystems later in more depth.

First generation: Coordinate large investments and build for scale

The Tech Community's ability to do what it does is hard earned. More than twenty years ago it was recognized that business was entering into a new age where sharing across companies would become central to success. Science and technology were progressing so quickly that most companies needed to focus their capital and talent narrowly to keep up, while simultaneously partnering with others to be effective.

Thus first generation business ecosystems were formed, which enabled networks of companies to coordinate large investments in research and development, capital equipment, and market development. Apple, Tandy, IBM, Intel and Microsoft made important contributions. This kind of partnering continued into mobile telephony and Internet development. Large investments were made in collaboration across companies. The industry learned many things, such as how to make contracts and protect valuable intellectual property while partnering with others, and how to join in shared financing when necessary to grow the ecosystems—for example, IBM invested $100m in Intel and helped Microsoft build its management systems. Later Intel invested in a variety of players in the ecosystem including Micron Technology in memory. Intel also invested generously in the open source and Linux communities, helping establish the second generation open business ecosystems.

The first generation ecosystems depended on a central player, which had an effective monopoly on its contributions and exerted its pricing power to achieve high margins, giving it large amounts of cash. It would exert its power over weaker firms in the ecosystem in order to assure alignment and coordination. In a May/June 1993 Harvard Business Review (HBR) piece I used the unfortunate but accurate term "choke-hold" for this role.[2] Marco Iansiti used the term "keystone" in his subsequent work on business ecosystems[3] and identified in clear terms the problems with force and inequality in ecosystems—that indeed a keystone could exert so much economic leverage that it could weaken and force out of business the very partners on which it depended. In the first business ecosystems coercive leadership was tolerated by ecosystem participants because there were few ecosystems available and it was much better to be in than out. For better or worse, the leadership styles in almost all first generation business ecosystems were broadly similar.

Second generation: Software, social networks and social movements

As experience in business ecosystems matured, it began to be widely appreciated that software as a product had a unique characteristic in that its replication cost almost nothing. If the first generation ecosystems leveraged property rights to support capital investment, a second generation of ecosystems emerged that eschewed property rights on intellectual property— "information wants to be free" — and promoted the benefits of open inclusive communities of knowledge sharing.

Proliferation over profits became the maxim as people discovered that software with millions of users was valuable and that software with few users was not. Computer networks evolved from primitive bulletin boards, chat rooms and instant messaging tools to Web and mobile-based social networking apps that stream text, audio and video content 24/7. With these technical platforms, communities were able to spread widely. Clay Shirky wrote of a cognitive surplus in society: there were lots of smart people who were under-engaged in their jobs and lives and longed to join with others and solve interesting challenges.[4] Networking and the open source movement developed this surplus into a powerful force for community building, learning and solving real problems. Yochai Benkler calls this "peer production"—a new and powerful input to our world economy.[5] The major product produced was software and computer networking, which in turn was a major enabler of further collaboration in a virtuous cycle of expanding participation.

With the advent of blogging, social networking and Twitter, the social power of second-generation ecosystems expanded. An example of this emerges in the political campaigns of the early 2000s, where politicians such as Vermont Governor Howard Dean began to amass real political power through social media. The Dean campaign gave way to the Obama campaign. Globally, the web and Twitter became the communications platform for the Arab Spring.

Third generation: capital-intensive flexible platforms enabling and enabled by social movements

If the first generation of ecosystems was about coordinating investment and the second generation was about streamlining the networks that enable us to collaborate and initiate social change, the third generation of business ecosystems emerged by combining the elements of both. The third generation of ecosystems saw the need and the opportunity of putting together the two earlier forms—a form that could manage and apply capital, and a form that could foment social movements and social change. This effect is seen most clearly in the most successful to date of the third generation form: the spreading ecology of smartphones.

The smartphone world involves some several thousand companies. The first thing I realized in researching this world is that it is not just one business ecosystem. There is no equivalent of the Microsoft Windows / Intel "Wintel" duopoly —though Apple and Samsung are quite powerful and Qualcomm has a high share of the core microprocessor and communications chips. What you have instead is what some members call the "connected community."

The connected community is a vast global collection of companies that are unified by a few standards and core technologies—ARM-designed microprocessors most visibly, but other complementary technologies as well, such as radios and signal processors. But what unifies them the most—and this is most fascinating—is a set of values about openness of ideas and technologies, treating each other well, and finding creative ways of profit sharing and risk mitigation so all members can thrive.

The connected community for smartphones depends on so-called "fabless" semiconductor companies such as Qualcomm and NVIDIA. Fabless companies design and sell chips, but they contract out the manufacturing to "foundries" including Samsung, Taiwan Semiconductor Manufacturing Company (known universally as TSMC), GlobalFoundries and others. These foundries do contract manufacturing at "fabs"—fabrication plants—and for all practical purposes are open to anyone who can pay them.

At the core of the connected community are the design disciplines. Electronic design automation—EDA—software translates high-level chip designs into instructions that in turn program computers that control manufacturing in the fabs. The electronic design for any given chip pulls together modular sub-designs from libraries, which in turn are "synthesized" into a master design—and then this design is refined and tested through many steps on the way to being tried in the fab. There are literally hundreds of firms that supply pieces of intellectual property that could be synthesized into a chip. These organizations range from cottage-industry companies, to complex EDA firms, to engineering groups inside the fabless semiconductor companies, to microprocessor design companies like ARM Holdings.

At the heart of this activity are the microprocessor design and licensing companies, with ARM Holdings having well above 95 percent share in smartphones. ARM designs and licenses microprocessor architectures that provide an overall order and orchestration for the design elements. The value of this architecture, among others, is that a shared architecture enables the industry to create a wide variety of chips and still have them run the same software and operate broadly interchangeably. ARM also sells its own intellectual property, both to feed modules into EDA synthesis, and to be used in conjunction with fabs for controlling physical processes. Most importantly, ARM has championed the open, networked ecosystem model that is the basis for the connected community and its many third generation ecosystems.

The connected community is most visible in the smartphone business. However it extends far beyond. There is a world of smart devices built on microprocessors that control everything from automotive engines, stability control, GPS and entertainment systems, to building controls for heating, lighting, security and fire protection. These processors are the brains of your cameras, the thermostat in your home, the medical devices you may depend on, and entertainment systems you enjoy. Coming soon is the so-called "Internet of things" — wearable, ingestible, implantable. One of my favorites is a type of chip that can be strewn into concrete by the hundreds as it is being poured, and that send out temperature readings that are used to determine if the concrete is curing properly.

The latest new frontier for the connected community is the data center and the servers that fill it. Servers are evolving quickly from racks of cards — each being a server — to racks of cards with dozens of servers on each — to, coming, banks of system-on-a-chips, SoCs, each comprising several microprocessors, linked together by the thousands. The data centers of the largest cloud companies — Facebook, Google, Microsoft and Amazon — are heading toward millions of servers. These in turn are being located in places where electricity is cheap—near hydroelectric dams in the Pacific Northwest, on the plains of Iowa where wind-power is plentiful. This market is the newest opportunity for the connected community and its myriad business ecosystems.

The culture and leadership of the connected community

As I began interviewing leaders of companies associated with ARM processors, I realized that I had dropped into a sub-culture of socially sophisticated, highly networked people, many of whom partook of the social values—the sharing and

6

collaborating—of the open source movement. They feel they are onto a very special approach to their work that functions well for business and is fun to boot. Camaraderie is a big part of open social movements after all.

The open source communities have developed what Eric Raymond calls "gift economies" and have a social psychology uniquely and powerfully their own: A culture of shared learning, shared work and shared products.[6]

Apply these ideas to a very large business sector—smartphones and the associated businesses that make up the connected community—and you have a worldwide revolution in business. The result is a social movement, a cultural milieu, an ethos and an extended community of tens of thousands of people.

Now layer on top of the worldwide-connected community a concept of business ecosystem that blends sharing and investment—the third generation ecosystem. In the rich growth medium of the connected community these business ecosystems multiply and interpenetrate, overlap and span.

The business ecosystem concept has become completely generalized. Every leader has at least one ecosystem and many have several. Business ecosystems are wrapped around products and services, they are used to solve technical problems, and they are used to open up markets. And of course they are used to bring app developers onto platforms. Business ecosystems are a widely understood social and business tool, applied at any scale for almost any shared purpose.

Leaders increasingly think in terms of multiple ecosystems. They look for ways in which two or more can strengthen each other, for example. As I got farther into my study, I realized that business ecosystems and their leaders sometimes travel in packs, hunting for opportunities together. An ARM ecosystem could join with a Dell ecosystem and a fabless semiconductor company in pursuing a lead for supplying data centers to Fidelity Investments. There is a third generation of business ecosystems, but there is in almost no meaningful sense an isolated third generation ecosystem. There is instead a complex, constantly changing topology of ecosystems.

Leadership lessons and the process of differentiated growth

As I asked for leadership lessons from across the connected community, I found a startling result. The leadership lessons were related to a set of roles being played in the community. And the roles, when seen together, formed a system for listening to customer pain and turning it into customer pull that in turn would organize a cross-community response and deliver an appropriate product.

The leaders, in their minds, were sitting "above" a landscape of customers and pain, companies, ecosystems and the connected community as a whole. They were occupied with monitoring and tweaking and developing a vast, sprawling worldwide "differentiation machine" that heard the cries of a myriad of customers in a multitude of settings. The machine generated in response a wild array of products and services. As the cries changed, as new markets opened up, the elements in the machine self-organized into new configurations to serve up new and different products.

Below are some of the key lessons in brief. In the following sections, each of these will be developed further:

1. Demand disruption

Sometimes technology stagnates and markets don't give us what we want. What can we do when this happens? Demand disruption! As a buyer we can insist that our suppliers form a collaborative, idea-sharing business ecosystem—with their direct rivals. We can insist that those who are central to the current industry do what they can to lower barriers to entry for newcomers. We can ask unthinkable things of our suppliers. We can demand better.

2. Explore beyond the edge

Business ecosystems form around problems to solve and pain to soothe. More problems are beyond the frontier of our current business landscape than within it. Nurture new business ecosystems beyond the frontier. Get to know the people beyond the edge, whose opportunities are cut short by problems we may be able to solve. Survey and map problems, catalogue the pain that needs to be relieved, understand the roots of pain. Connect new customers with new partners to create new ecosystems in new places.

3. Reach to everyone

Liberate powerful technologies from the few. Let everyone gain access to technology and expand their personal opportunities. Applied technology enriches daily life, saves labor and reduces costs and risks. As technologists we know this from personal experience. To reach a wider range of customers we can design our business ecosystems to produce a range of products, prices, benefits and tradeoffs. Differentiate our offerings, be flexible in our options and diversify whom we serve.

4. Wrap an ecosystem around every product and service

Every product and service is also a marketplace for further products and services that enrich the opportunities customers can pursue. We provide value by selecting and recruiting these resources, categorizing, testing and certifying them. We are in prime position to collect and publish customer feedback, continuously improving the ecosystem. When we increase the access of members to each other by making markets we increase productive exchanges. Increasing exchanges creates more value faster and advances the whole.

5. Draw deeply from science and engineering

Science and engineering are the most fundamental inputs to innovation in a business ecosystem. University and private labs are rich sources of ideas. Bringing an idea forward requires a team of experts including those who understand the discovery and those who know the industrial situation. The typical time frame for moving a discovery out of the lab to market is a decade or more. Our business ecosystems must have at their core processes of science translation — Bell Lab's "reduction to practice" — where people can work closely, in secret, at the highest professional levels, for a decade or more. This is in fact what does happen in our best ecosystems, an incredible feat little appreciated beyond the inner walls.

6. Take just enough

Greed spoils business ecosystems. Open ecosystems are gift economies that depend on reciprocal care. They require considering a situation from all sides. Get clear on a fundamental choice: you can grow your business by growing the ecosystem and advancing the opportunities for your customer. You can also grow a business — at least in terms of revenues and profits — by taking from your ecosystem and from your customers. The philosophy of "just enough" is not about austerity. Indeed, those in the connected community are thriving. It is caring about your partners, not "sucking the life out of them" by exerting your bargaining power when they are weaker. It is about gaining your security and your enjoyment and your accomplishments with others — in ways that are sustainable as a business, organization and person.

7. Open it

The human, technical and economic benefits of open ecosystems and the connected community are so dramatic that it seems nothing can stop it. On the other hand, a problem internal to the community itself might be posed by the actions of a rogue operator — for example a patent trc!l or hostile takeover opportunist. In an open, connected economy, the role of senior leaders includes being alert for challenges to the integrity of the community and leading preemptive, corrective or defensive action as necessary. Overall, the connected community and its ecosystems are growing, scaling and differentiating as organizations. This provides an opportunity for new forms of co-leadership across the community.

8. I thou

Emotional intelligence is perhaps the most important attribute of effective members of an open business ecosystem. Professional expertise matters a great deal, but if not expressed with maturity and care, the close relationships on which the ecosystem depends cannot function. Human resources strategies can be designed to recruit, train, motivate and promote those with emotional intelligence. The Jewish philosopher Martin Buber presented this idea well. He said we can treat each other and ourselves as an "it" — as objects to be driven, threatened, used. Or we can treat each other as "thou" — persons to be respected, cared for, learned from, with values, creativity and giftedness.[7]

NOTES

[1] Williamson, Oliver E., 2007. "Transaction Cost Economics: An Introduction," Economics Discussion Papers 2007-3, Kiel Institute for the World Economy.

[2] "Predators and Prey: A new ecology of competition" James F. Moore, Harvard Business Review, May/June 1993

[3] The Keystone Advantage: What the New Dynamics of Business Ecosystems Mean for Strategy, Innovation and Sustainability, Marco Iansiti and Roy Levien, Harvard Business School Press, 2004

[4] Cognitive Surplus: Creativity and Generosity in a Connected Age, Clay Shirky, Penguin Books, 2010

[5] The Wealth of Networks: How Social Production Transforms Markets and Freedom, Yochai Benkler, Free Press, 2006

[6] The Cathedral & the Bazaar: Musings on Linux and open source by an accidental revolutionary, Eric S. Raymond, O'Reilly Media, 1999

[7] I and Thou, Martin Buber, 1923, English trans. 1937

Demand disruption

Sometimes technology stagnates and markets don't give us what we want. What can we do when this happens? Demand disruption! As a buyer we can insist that our suppliers form a collaborative, idea-sharing business ecosystem—with their direct rivals. We can insist that those who are central to the current industry do what they can to lower barriers to entry for newcomers. We can ask unthinkable things of our suppliers. We can demand better.

•

Facebook, Applied Micro, Calxeda and Red Hat

•

Frank Frankovsky is head of hardware at Facebook. He is a big, bearded man who lives in Austin, Texas. He spends a good deal of time at Facebook headquarters in Menlo Park, California. He has problems with his server farms — well, to start with he'd rather they not be either "farms" or contain conventional "servers." He wants to "break up the monolith" of server architecture — so that fast-evolving parts such as microprocessors are interchangeable, while slower-moving parts such as communications channels are only changed as needed.

Frankovsky is initiating a business ecosystem called the Open Compute Project.[1] He has a vision of where he wants to go and how he wants to measure success. His current thinking is summed up in "Group Hug" — which includes taking what is today on a motherboard — which evolves slowly — and standardizing its functions and its interfaces. This will in turn enable microprocessors to be switched out when they become obsolete — which is quickly — without replacing other perfectly adequate parts of the system.

Frank has invited a number of companies to the table, and many others have shown up — at least 50 companies smell a rich opportunity. Frank wants it this way, he wants to encourage investment by coming as close as possible to assuring that if they build it he will buy. He ideally wants more than just better products. He would like the companies he is involved with to collaborate and move toward open ecosystem models.

Frank is exploring how far he can go toward an open source collaboration model for hardware companies. He points out that the current model for open source communities is suited for software, because individuals can make substantial contributions as short-term volunteers.

> *"In an open software ecosystem an individual's passion and an individual's skill and talent is almost all you need. A software engineer can change the world with a few nights of coding. Their contribution is their intellectual property and their time.*

> *"Whereas in the hardware ecosystem we have tangible infrastructure that needs to be built and that requires tangible dollars."*

He and I share an interest in hybrid ecosystems that combine open and commercial models, such as the ARM ecosystem.

Frank said,

> *"We are still exploring what open source looks like in the hardware ecosystem. How open can it be, how collaborative can it be and where does there need to be more traditional property rights so that people who engage in the ecosystem can build a reasonable commercial opportunity out of this?*

> *"This is an area that fascinates me. We hope to break down some barriers with Open Compute.*

> *"When we established the IP policies we leveraged the Open Web Foundation agreements—clearly oriented towards software.*

> *"But then one of the founding members of Open Compute is Intel."*

Frank went on to say how Open Compute and Intel had worked together on a model copyright agreement so that Intel — and others — could contribute specific intellectual property while drawing a boundary around it. Then the agreement was shared with other members, and because Intel's legal department had agreed to it, other companies were inclined to believe it would protect their interests.

> *"It's still far from frictionless but we are seeing some amount of change. I will give you a great example. Intel has invested for more than a decade in the silicone photonics technology.*

13

"Thinking and talking about open sourcing that technology was a very interesting discussion. I don't want to speak for them but from my perspective the reason that they came forward what because they saw the benefit of how quickly Open Compute could make that technology pervasive."

I noted that, counter-intuitively, Frank is not asking his suppliers to lower their prices or to make better products, he is asking them to open up to a new model of sharing. And he is trying to convince them that this is in their best interests — for example, to open up in order to have their technology proliferate.

"They are not open sourcing the process technology that allows them to provide photonics and silicone, which is their core intellectual property.

"But they open sourced the connector so that anybody in the ecosystem can download the specifications and develop a product around the photonics.

"So that's a sign of things to come. Intel obviously has a lot to protect. And even they are thinking differently about this ecosystem. I think they see that the world is changing and business models are changing."[2]

By early 2013 four companies had built and demonstrated hardware that allowed processors to be supported interchangeably — Intel, AMD — both X86 architecture — and AppliedMicro and Calxeda, representing ARM architecture. Intel engineers have come up with a socket design that is processor agnostic, and all four are using it. What this means is that as Facebook continues to advance toward implementing its new server architecture it will start to put ARM vendors on a precisely equivalent hardware footing with Intel and AMD.

Why would Facebook do this? While continuing to work with Intel and AMD, Facebook wants access to the diversity of the full connected community and its ecosystems. Today Facebook has two new suppliers, AppliedMicro and Calxeda, tomorrow it will have more, the next day even more. Frank is holding open the door to invite new ideas and talent into his data centers.

The ever-differentiated ARM ecosystem has in Applied Micro and Calxeda two very different approaches to a server processor — two different bets. Both will be made available to Facebook. Applied Micro has an ARM architecture license and is making an ultra-high-performance processor. In raw performance it is designed to roughly equal a top Intel processor, but be more power-efficient.

Applied Micro is headquartered in Sunnyvale the Silicon Valley, a dozen miles south of Facebook's headquarters in Menlo Park. Paramesh Gopi is the colorful CEO of Applied Micro. He equated his goal to building the BMW of ARM chips,

> *"What we're driving toward is optimal performance—the ultimate driving machine."*

Picking up the bait, I said,

> *"So you're a BMW, not a Prius."*

Paramesh said,

> *"Exactly, I think we should talk about us more as a Lexus 450 hybrid —or a Lexus GS hybrid."[3]*

That is, a luxury car with plenty of power and interior passenger space, and with the ability to run on electric power when appropriate. Later he spends several minutes explaining that in order to succeed in the large-scale server and data center market, ARM partners will have to match the cadence of the existing cloud data center ecosystem. Paramesh notes that his offering is intended to do just that, to be an easy upgrade, and once having entered the cloud world Applied Micro will add further differentiation away from Intel and AMD.

Meanwhile from their headquarters in silvery cylinder on the west side of Austin, Texas, Calxeda's Karl Freund explained their approach.

> *"We don't want to be almost as good as an Intel Xeon, we want to be different."*

Different in the Calxeda case is putting together many ARM processors tied together by a special energy-efficient connecting fabric. They see themselves at the beginning of their evolution; right now Calxeda chips can handle light jobs such as file serving, and do it power-efficiently. The fabric and the processors come as a unit that can be made interchangeable with the most common Intel chips used in data centers like Facebook.

> *"Customers like us because of our open business model and ARM's open model."*

At the highest level, Calxeda's promise is that they will innovate for and with the customer and that they have access to solution elements that are potentially powerful. Karl goes as far as to tell customers,

> *"We are probably not the only choice for you. You may decide to buy from us for certain applications and buy from Applied Micro for others. What we can assure you is that in either case the software will be compatible. Once you set yourself up to use any ARM systems, the*

15

diversified ARM ecosystem will continue to expand the options available to you."[4]

A couple weeks later I stepped into a funky Cambridge, Massachusetts coffee house a few blocks from MIT. Jon Masters of Red Hat was already there. He's a regular, and he was chatting up the person behind the counter as she made his coffee. We tucked ourselves into the back corner booth. Jon is an ultra-high energy computer scientist who is the chief ARM architect at Red Hat, the open source Linux company. We talk about Facebook, Open Compute and the two ARM companies.

Jon said,

> *"Both companies are taking different approaches, [Applied Micro] are doing a custom design — very fast, very high end 64-bit Encore in the next technology generation. Calxeda are going to also have a 64-bit design but the difference is Calxeda are not doing a custom core design. Their value is about integrating fabric across the chips."*

Red Hat will support both, though it currently only supports ARM through its experimental Fedora version.

For Red Hat, an open ecosystem is a mixed blessing. It currently can focus on a single architecture. This simplifies business. On the other hand, he sees how this simplification has held back progress.

> *"We've [the IT space] had a convenience in the last decade or so where we've had certain large players that have had a strategic stronghold in the market. And good for them, they've done great. But lack of competition is why we're looking at things like hyper scale computing now and not five years ago. Fast-forward five or ten years from now you're going to see a much more dynamic marketplace."[5]*

Jon is enthusiastic about Frank's initiative because it is accelerating the opening.

Stepping back from AppliedMicro and Calxeda, one can see how effective Frankovsky's ecosystem initiative may be. It already has managed to press Intel and the three other firms to agree to make their processors interchangeable. It has added two creative and very different voices to the table. It is establishing communication among companies that would not normally talk, and it is forcing each one to pay attention to the others.

Facebook is an example of a powerful customer insisting that its vendors form an ecosystem around its priorities. It is not alone. Companies like Fidelity

Investments are also looking for custom data center designs. A highly differentiated ecosystem with lots of companies will find a way to serve them. And on the telecommunications side, large carriers like AT&T and BT are joining a Network Functions Virtualization[6] project to encourage ecosystems for software defined networking, so that infrastructure is open and interchangeable.

The promotion of business ecosystems by large, powerful buyers almost guarantees disruptive results if the talent can be held together, because it encourages new people with new ideas, new money, new tools and new technologies. Customers give the newcomers precious information about their problems and they promise a market. I look forward to staying tuned to these stories.

More generally there is a theme here that I'd like to apply to my own professional and personal life. I can ask, "How can I work with those who supply me to encourage them to become open to new ideas and new contributors, so that in the long run I'm served by a more vibrant, more diverse and multiparty ecosystem?"

We all put up with things that make no sense, in both our professional and personal lives. Rather than putting up with it, can we use our buying power to encourage open ecological change? If our own buying power and power of persuasion is not enough, can we band together with still others to increase our collective clout? Can we form customer-led, change-making ecosystems? Can we establish ecosystems to promote open ecosystems? I'm inspired that Frank Frankovsky at Facebook is doing this and having some effect and learning a great deal.

NOTES

[1] Open Compute Project, http://www.opencompute.org

[2] Frank Frankovsky, Facebook, personal communication, February 2013

[3] Paramesh Gopi, Applied Micro, personal communication, February 2013

[4] Karl Freund, Calxeda, personal communication, February 2013

[5] Jon Masters, Red Hat, personal communication, March 2013

[6] "Leading operators create ETSI standards group for network functions virtualization," ETSI, January 22, 2013 http://www.etsi.org/news-events/news/644-2013-01-isg-nfv-created

Explore beyond the edge

B
usiness ecosystems form around problems to solve and pain to soothe. More problems are beyond the frontier of our current business landscape than within it. Nurture new business ecosystems beyond the frontier. Get to know the people beyond the edge, whose opportunities are cut short by problems we may be able to solve. Survey and map problems, catalogue the pain that needs to be relieved, understand the roots of pain. Connect new customers with new partners to create new ecosystems in new places.

•

Dell, Xilinx, ARM Holdings, Nicole St. Claire Knobloch, Bill Gates

•

Bill Gates authored an opinion piece in the Wall Street Journal this January. His topic was metrics. His title was "My Plan to Fix the World's Biggest Problems."[1] He began by sharing an article on the development of steam power — a 19th century analogue to the semiconductor industry.

> *"We can learn a lot about improving the 21st-century world from an icon of the industrial era: the steam engine.*
>
> *"Harnessing steam power required many innovations, as William Rosen chronicles in the book 'The Most Powerful Idea in the World.' Among the most important were a new way to measure the energy output of engines and a micrometer dubbed the "Lord Chancellor" that could gauge tiny distances.*
>
> *"Such measuring tools, Mr. Rosen writes, allowed inventors to see if their incremental design changes led to the improvements — such as higher power and less coal consumption — needed to build better engines. There's a larger lesson here: Without feedback from precise measurement, Mr. Rosen writes, invention is 'doomed to be rare and erratic.' With it, invention becomes 'commonplace'."*

Gates went on to discuss the power of the UN Millennium Goals and their (to many) surprising effectiveness in guiding shared action on the world's biggest

19

problems. Goal number four, reducing childhood mortality worldwide, embodies a metric that is simple — how many children died this year? — and yet in order to move the needle requires a multitude of integrated contributions toward the shared goal.

Public health as a field has become skilled at focusing on specific strategic measures--witness the success of controlling most infectious diseases and eliminating smallpox and — almost — polio. Business ecosystems need the same focus on strategic, industry-wide objectives. Interestingly, recently the focus on reducing electric power in information technology has begun to take on characteristics of a broad shared goal that integrates a variety of contributions.

Childhood deaths have declined dramatically over the two decades of campaigns to address it.

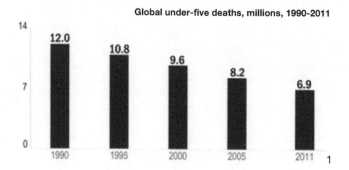

Global under-five deaths, millions, 1990-2011

Source: Unicef http://www.childinfo.org/mortality_underfive.php

Shared goals move the world because they inspire us in addition to providing orientation. Technology in particular rewards dedication, persistence and creativity, as well as — usually — working for team credit and suppressing one's ego. Big, well-considered goals motivate the best people; e.g. X Prizes, grand challenges, the campaign to eradicate smallpox, and the campaign to reduce child deaths.

A story from ARM Holdings begins many years ago when a major partner wanted chips for mobile phones. This company suggested ARM limit its processor to a 250-milliwatt budget for electrical power — tiny by computer standards — and asked that ARM learn how to double the processing capability of chips every 18 months while keeping power constant. Of course ARM could have rejected this technology strategy but, by embracing it, ARM learned how to

20

do sophisticated power saving in advance of its competitors. This in turn helped the entire ecosystem to succeed with small devices of all kinds, and energy efficiency is today one of ARM's most distinctive competencies.[2]

The point is that co-evolving with a customer to tackle a difficult customer problem — and persisting at it — can be a surprisingly reliable, if patience-requiring, route to acquiring unique capabilities and entering new markets.

The theme of fixing on targets outside of our reach, of aiming at goals beyond the frontier of business as usual, is needed more and more today. Business ecosystems seem to work best when they are chartered and measured by broad important goals. And once these goals have been set, there is nothing like the field of practice for figuring out how to proceed.

My adopted hometown of Concord, Massachusetts is the sort of place where strangers strike up conversations, and often the result is surprisingly relevant. On my way back to my writing office from dinner (bean salad and strong coffee at a little French cafe near the train station), I stopped in the local bookstore, thinking I might get some ideas. I found a book and struck up a conversation with a person working behind the counter named Nicole St. Claire Knobloch.[3]

We started talking about business leadership and the environment and she seemed quite plugged in. Turns out she is a global warming expert and activist who has worked for major environmental groups in Washington, for think tanks, and for Ford Motor Company. Frustrated with both lack of progress and (in her view) the lack of effectiveness of the environmental movement, she is temporarily holed up near Concord writing a magazine article on a theory of change for the environmental movement. There is local Concord precedent for writing about social change and the environment. Henry David Thoreau's Walden is the swimming pond most frequented by local kids, Ralph Waldo Emerson's house is right around the corner from Main Street.

I asked if she could summarize her theory of change. She demurred, but when encouraged a bit more explained that the large systems that need changing in relation to global warming — such as energy and transportation — have systemic trigger points for change. These (my words) pain points identify places where new technologies and new operating and business models are needed.

I quickly asked her if she had a map of these trigger points. Yes — but unfortunately only a partial map. She recognizes that she needs help in mapping and analysis, and in part her writing is aimed at syndicating her method.

I mentioned that I had been on the phone earlier that day with two executives from a company who were talking about growing their business ecosystem. Their leadership model includes mapping "pain points" across a target territory in a systematic and comprehensive way. Once the pattern of pain has been identified, the company helps attract in partners that may have solutions. Often the solution comes from small, specialist companies, and the larger company may need to invest in or otherwise assist the company in bringing its solution to maturity and integrating it into the ecosystem. I did not mention it to her, but the company is Xilinx and the ecosystem surrounds their Smarter Vision Initiative. I was speaking with Steve Glaser and Dave Tokic, to be returned to in a later chapter.[4]

Across the connected community, leaders from CEOs, to segment marketing leaders, to heads of ecosystem development are focused on identifying systems of pain points facing their customers and their customers' customers — who might include big vertical players like an auto company — or could be a large cloud service provider like Baidu or a telecom company like China Mobile.

One way to think about this is as a process of sensing, amplifying and organizing to be responsive to customer pull. Authors John Hagel, John Seely Brown and Lang Davison in the excellent book The Power of Pull highlight the vitality and longevity of businesses that create and respond to pull, over those who primarily push. [5] In a world of fast-changing customer and market conditions, with a diversity that makes a single solution hard to sell, pull comes out ahead. The connected community before us is designed to amplify market pull from a multitude of sources. In particular, a great deal of management time and attention is invested in proactively seeking out pull from beyond the edges of its comfort zone, from markets and customers beyond its current frontiers. A constant, core-of-the-business effort to find pain points and turn them into pull and response is at the foundation of how the community expands.

Perhaps even more interesting, there seems to be a community of — for lack of a better word-explorers beyond the frontier, that spans companies and enables ad hoc conversations, working groups and small ecosystems to be assembled in response to pain and customer pull.

I like the story of how in 2007 Robert Hormuth of Dell made a breakthrough in understanding the customer pain about the electricity consumption of server farms and data centers. It was common knowledge that usage was rising fast. But how, he asked, could he get under the problem and get a handle on addressing it?

He suspected that much server power might be wasted running big chips at idle. After all, a good bit of the storage load that servers access is so-called "cold storage" of "cold data" — seldom needed but important to keep accessible. It did not seem possible that this class of computing, at least, needed powerful chips. He commissioned a study.

> *"The results were surprising and shocking,"* said Hormuth. *"They don't need all the horsepower being thrown at them. They were just sitting there using up watts."*[6]

He began to wonder if cell phone chips, obviously power misers, could be made into web servers. Robert had formerly been at Intel, and Ian Drew, a colleague and friend of his from Intel, was now head of marketing at ARM in the UK. Robert called him, which led quickly to plans for a meeting with Robert, Ian Drew and Ian Ferguson of ARM. Ian Ferguson's job at the time was to live out beyond the edge, on the frontier among the big server users, and find pain, make friends and look for opportunity. At the time Ian Ferguson displayed the following self-description on the ARM directory web site:

> *Ian Ferguson... has spent years fighting from the corner of the underdog. Most of those scars are healing nicely. Ian is particularly passionate about taking ARM technology into new types of applications that do not exist or are at the very formative stages. Consequently, he is driving ARM's server program with a view to reinvent the way the server function is implemented in networks as opposed to simply replacing incumbent platforms.*[7]

Late in 2007 Robert flew to Los Angeles to make a meeting happen among the three of them, and a small but very serious initiative was born.[8] Chip design, development, licensing manufacturing is a multi-year process. The first thing that needed to be ascertained was when the capability of ARM-based chips would cross the threshold needed for servers. Second, what if any special features might need to be added to the basic chip design. For this second task, a server was set up running an obviously inadequate processor, but enough to identify any key limitations and suggest design tweaks. Third, what was the plan for an ecosystem? Dell does not make its chips, and it preferred more than one vendor.

Robert explains that as Dell and ARM got deeper into discussions they both put an emphasis on

> *"enabling more interest in an ecosystem — a fast paced ecosystem that provided our customers and us more choice."*[9]

Dell and ARM began to work as a system to convert loud sounds of pain on the part of customers into a plan. The heart of the plan was to specify — and amplify — problems clearly so they could be understood by a cross-company, cross-department ad hoc ecosystem. Many partners would be involved: the ARM architecture group, the fabs and tool community, and the fabless semiconductor companies that would ultimately oversee designing and making the server chips.

There is method to this madness beyond the frontier. In China, for example, ARM has a team whose only job is to make connections among entrepreneurs in the tech space, accelerating commerce. Of course in the process it develops a comprehensive and nuanced understanding of local pain, players and priorities.

Ian Ferguson has now moved up a level and oversees a dozen teams like his former group in servers, all working beyond one frontier or another.

> *"ARM's role in the chemical reaction is to be the catalyst. So, you'd sprinkle a little bit of magic pixie dust, and ... then ... it's really the rest of the ecosystem."*[10]

He tries to sprinkle pixie dust evenly, and then get out of the scene. He tries not to influence the outcome. Only by doing this can he maintain the trust of ARM partners, and that of the prospective customer.

He described a recent situation where two of ARM's server partners were introduced to a prospective customer, but only one would win. He stepped back and let the competition run. One won and one lost. I asked him if there were hard feelings and he said,

> *"No, because both know that I'm even handed, and they know this is just one of many introductions and competitions, and they expect to win their share."*[11]

The lesson here is that growth can be achieved by systematic work beyond the edge. That work requires patience and tends to have a very long, multi-year gestation time. And the story of Robert Hormuth and Dell does not stand alone. At any given time any number of nascent ecosystems are being nurtured. Having a process of pioneering is essential to successfully bringing together group after group of lead customers, helpful allies, experts within and outside of the connected community, and entrepreneurs.

Finally, the connected community has a variety of members and ecosystems it can introduce potential partner to, each providing something different. In the next section we will emphasize customers whose needs can be met — at least in part — out of the enormous range of pre-existing technology available from partners. This is particularly true in the microcontroller and small device market, where flexibility, low cost and immediate delivery rule.

Overall, the connected community is designed to produce choice for customers and differentiation for producers, as we will examine in the next chapter.

NOTES

1 "My Plan to Fix The World's Biggest Problems," Bill Gates, The Wall Street Journal, January 25, 2013

2 Ian Thornton, ARM Holdings, personal communication, November 2012

3 Nicole St. Claire Knobloch, Concord Bookshop, Concord, MA, personal communication, April 2013

4 Steve Glaser and Dave Tokic, Xilinx, April 2013

5 John Hagel III, John Seely Brown: Lang Davison, The Power of Pull: How Small Moves, Smartly Made, Can Set Big Things In Motion, Basic Books 2010.

6 Robert Hormuth, Dell, quoted in "ARM Muscles in on Intel's Dominance in Datacenters." HPCWire High Performance Computing, January 28, 2013

7 Ian Ferguson profile, ARM Community Network, 2012-2013
http://forums.arm.com/index.php?/user/104715-ian-ferguson/

8 Robert Hormuth, Dell, personal communication, April 2013

9 Ibid.

10 Ian Ferguson, personal communication, April 2013

11 Ian Ferguson profile, ARM Community Network, 2012-2013
http://forums.arm.com/index.php?/user/104715-ian-ferguson/

Reach to everyone

L iberate powerful technologies from the few. Let everyone gain access to technology and expand their personal opportunities. Applied technology enriches daily life, saves labor and reduces costs and risks. As technologists we know this from personal experience. To reach a wider sphere of customers we can design our business ecosystems to produce a range of products, prices, benefits and tradeoffs. Differentiate our offerings, be flexible in our options and diversify whom we serve.

•

DIY Drones, Freescale Semiconductors, Harvard University

•

In 2007 Chris Anderson, the editor of Wired Magazine, founded a Do It Yourself (DIY) community to make personal drones. There had long been a worldwide hobbyist community making and flying model airplanes — but these were not autonomous. They were tethered — either by actual physical lines or by radio control units. What they lacked was the ability to fly by themselves free from tether. Anderson's insight was that the control technology to enable reliable long-range drones was becoming available at a price many could afford — in the range of a few hundred dollars. As he put it in an article last summer,

> *"Just as the 1970s saw the birth and rise of the personal computer, this decade will see the ascendance of the personal drone. We're entering the Drone Age."*[1]

A business ecosystem is initiated by bringing together the fruits of science with the needs of society. In less formal terms, entrepreneurs liberate technologies and make them widely available. William Gibson's famous statement that *"the future is already here, it's just not evenly distributed yet"*[2] is not just an observation. It also poses implicit questions: "Why isn't the future distributed yet? What would happen if it was?" And most exhilarating: "Do you think we might be able to do it — to let the future loose?" Wearable computers, ingestible sensors, wireless communications from inside the body, personal drones — the real lesson of the past decade or so is that the public itself, including hobbyists, DIY "makers," kids in school and out, will spread the word and distribute the future.

27

You don't achieve this just by extending Moore's law — by simply going smaller, denser and faster.[3] That would be like attributing all the blessings of modern transportation to the advancement of metallurgy or internal combustion. Moore's law is necessary but not sufficient. The new business ecosystems have an explicit intent to let people communicate knowledge among themselves and to liberate useful technologies. They have gained this in part from the social fruits of the open-source movement and from the social networking experience in general. This social experience is joined with something I consider an essential and often unnoticed fruit of the first-generation ecosystems: modular and flexible components that can be put together to perform sophisticated functions by (relatively) unsophisticated makers. It was the modularity of electronic components that let the two Steves — Jobs and Wozniak — build a "phone phreaking" device to trick Bell System computers into allowing free long distance calls. They sold their "blue box" in the dorms of UC Berkeley, and subsequently, building on this experience, created and sold the personal computer.

The new generation ecosystems are explicitly designed for freedom, choice and flexibility — for sensing and satisfying customer pull. I often think we need a new "law of flexibility" to complement and build on Moore's law. The more that Moore's law takes us deeper into the atomic level, the more theoretical flexibility we have to redesign and reconstruct our world. The great physicist Richard Feynman pointed this out years ago in a lecture that is widely viewed as founding the nanosciences. In an after-dinner speech to the American Physical Society in 1957, Feynman said,

> *"At the atomic level, we have new kinds of forces and new kinds of possibilities, new kinds of effects. The problems of manufacture and reproduction of materials will be quite different. I am, as I said, inspired by the biological phenomena in which chemical forces are used in a repetitious fashion to produce all kinds of weird effects (one of which is the author)."[4]*

Great combinatorial diversity is born of having more pieces to combine. As the size of pieces approaches the atomic level, the possible combinations approach infinity. The phenomenon holds at other scales. For example, a useful discussion of this phenomenon at the ecosystem level is "Population diversity and ecosystem services," a widely referenced paper by Gary Luck, Gretchen Daily and Paul Ehrlich of Stanford.[5] They attempt to measure "ecosystem services" — that is, the services provided by ecosystems to those within and beyond their borders. We can think of this as the analogue of services a business ecosystem provides in response to a variety of customer pulls. The variety of services depends on the variety of organisms making up the ecosystem, and the ability of these organisms to join in unique and useful combinations.

The success of the smartphone is just one dimension of a much broader Cambrian-explosion of diverse products. I consider this expansion of diversity every bit as fundamental as Moore's law, even as it builds on that earlier law. Maybe we should name it after whoever is best able to quantify it. Gordon Moore's original paper is a serious piece of scientific observation and insight. Moore himself anticipated the issue of flexibility in his 1965 paper, and thought about it as a way to share the cost of achieving continuing advances in leading edge manufacturing.

"Clearly, we will be able to build such component-crammed equipment. Next, we ask under what circumstances we should do it. The total cost of making a particular system function must be minimized. To do so, we could amortize the engineering over several identical items, or evolve flexible techniques for the engineering of large functions so that no disproportionate expense need be borne by a particular array. Perhaps newly devised design automation procedures could translate from logic diagram to technological realization without any special engineering.

"It may prove to be more economical to build large systems out of smaller functions, which are separately packaged and interconnected. The availability of large functions, combined with functional design and construction, should allow the manufacturer of large systems to design and construct a considerable variety of equipment both rapidly and economically."[6]

Fast-forward five decades to today, and Moore's vision is being realized. Consider Freescale Semiconductor, a global semiconductor company that sells inexpensive, power-efficient flexibility with more-than-good-enough speed. Freescale manufactures and sells a dizzying range of chips packaged and ready to be interconnected, most of them available off-the-shelf through online distributors such as Mouser Electronics. Mouser lists hundreds of Freescale products, most selling for far less than $100.[7] One of these products soon to hit the market is a tiny microcontroller 1.9 x 2 mm that Mouser says is [8]"with great potential for ... portable consumer devices, remote sensing nodes, wearable devices and ingestible healthcare sensing."

I spoke with Geoff Lees and Mario Centeno of Freescale. Geoff leads the microcontrollers business and Mario is a senior executive in strategy. They are based in Austin, Texas, home of the South by Southwest Music Festival as well as fabulous BBQ ribs.

I asked them how Freescale is able to offer such a wildly diverse range of chips, almost all at markedly low prices. The answer: Gordon Moore's 1965 hope that "design automation procedures could translate from logic diagram to technological realization without any special engineering" has largely been accomplish by an ecosystem of independent electronic design automation companies and their partners. Freescale is a sponsor, customer and beneficiary of this achievement, and manufactures chips at fabs around the world.

As Geoff explained,

> "In the mid-2000s we began to see a trend toward using automated design software to pull together software models representing, say, one or more microprocessors plus a number of other functions, and then use the design software to 'synthesize' the models into instructions to drive the manufacturing line in a fab, down to the molecular level.

> "So EDA companies such as Cadence, Synopsys take a high-level language and synthesize it into actual real world physical logic.

> "Automation in hardware design made small-run, specialized chips economically viable. A newly expanded range of customers could be offered specialty chips at affordable prices.

> "It's clear that the hardware side of our industry has reached a level of efficiency that [allows us to] deliver flexible hardware solutions at the right price and the right power and the right profile for customers. And that differentiation is now."

Variety can now be achieved without exotic processes and unaffordable fabs. Geoff is an admirer of what Intel accomplished in pursuit of a linear Moore's law, and what their work taught the world. On the other hand, he sees that most of what customers desire today can be achieved without exotic processes — including the tiny Internet-of-things devices presaged by his 2mm processor.

> "Everything we are doing now is focused on lower power. Extracting the best performance in power out of conventional silicon solutions, spread over many, many foundries, over many partners. It's really going to fuel these devices."[9]

In two years we will celebrate the 50th anniversary of Moore's paper. It is time we created a rigorous, well-publicized way to measure the advance of flexibility and design freedom so that we can celebrate our successes and motivate creativity.

In order to kick off the celebration, here are some notable contributions to flexibility and choice:

- A spirit that encourages differentiation. Human values, personal relationships and sustainable lives form the basis for professional partnerships. These partnerships in turn encourage the best and most distinctive contributions by each partner to the whole. This spirit extends to customers and encourages variety within the customer community, and helps customers guide ecosystem creativity.

- Tools, components and programmability for flexibility. In order to advance the frontier of differentiation, make use of advances in design automation software combined with modularity and programmability in key components: Field Programmable Gate Arrays, Application Specific Integrated Circuits, multi-capability chips (e.g. six types of radios available and baked on the chip), and custom-designed and manufactured chips.

- Rules designed as platforms for variety. Adopt architectures and standards that enable differentiation rather than enforce uniformity. Encourage community problem-solving that is self-reflective on this matter, so that the judgment of community members grows with the platforms themselves.

- Common resources open to a variety of uses. Make substantial contributions to the common base of technology on which the ecosystem lives. Examples include the Common Platform Initiative enabling IBM, Samsung and GlobalFoundries to make leading-edge manufacturing available through a foundry model. At the software end of the spectrum, collaborative initiatives like the open-source Linaro initiative are developing shared flexibility-enhancing "middleware" to help bring new applications onto a range of hardware.

- Appropriate technology diversity matching desired results. Take advantage of the variation in manufacturing capability across the ecosystem. Each time the leading edge in fabrication moves ahead, factories that only recently were seen as state-of-the-art are made available to a wider user base. The equipment and the fab are paid for. The people are experienced and the processes have been refined. Implementation is straightforward and safe compared to the leading edge, design automation tools are mature and the yield of useable chips is likely to be comparatively high.

Taken together these contributions — and no doubt more I don't know about — lower the cost and expertise barriers, enhance flexibility, increase choice up and down the value chain including for the end customer and application designer, and enable the ecosystem to expand into an ever larger array of markets.

They also give the lie to the widely held view that because leading-edge fabs are becoming more and more expensive, chip technology is becoming less and less accessible to small companies and to members of open ecosystems. The opposite is true. Because of concerted industry investments in democratization, open access and low barriers to entry, flexibility — or the law named after whoever is able to quantify this advancing frontier — continues to progress at a rate equal to and perhaps greater than Moore's law. The world needs the moon shots, the U.S. government-funded Defense Advanced Research Projects Administration (DARPA) investments, and the relentless Intel and IBM pursuit of the frontier. But as these investments pay off, the knowledge they yield and the technology they leave in their wake are free for the populace to take up and distribute. I conclude with Chris Anderson again:

> *"Today, all the sensors required to make a functioning autopilot have become radically smaller and radically cheaper. Gyroscopes, which measure rates of rotation; magnetometers, which function as digital compasses; pressure sensors, which measure atmospheric pressure to calculate altitude; accelerometers, to measure the force of gravity — all the capabilities of these technologies are now embedded in tiny chips that you can buy at RadioShack. Indeed, some of the newest sensors combine three-axis accelerometers, gyros, and magnetometers (nine sensors in all), plus a temperature gauge and a processor, into one little package that costs about $17.[10]*

This is choice, flexibility and access. RadioShack is the exemplar of Feynman's law.

Postscript:

The accessibility revolution is not limited to semiconductors, and appears wherever the manipulation of atoms and molecules is valuable. J.D. Deng manages Harvard's Laboratory of Integrated Science and Engineering, a facility open to students with several clean rooms and extensive but small-scale Nano fabrication and Nano imaging capabilities. Mostly the work is focused on Nano-Bio. Last fall I took an evening extension course with J.D. We made sensors with carbon nanotubes that measured about a nanometer across and were "instrumented" (impregnated) with gold Nano particles. You can buy these instrumented nanotubes at lab supply houses. We attached the nanotubes to silicon dioxide wafers by weak intermolecular forces (van der Waals forces). We checked our work with atomic force microscopes capable of imaging a molecule. The microscopes fit on a desktop and cost a few thousand dollars.

J.D.'s course is complemented by one on microfluidics, labs-on-a-chip and soft lithography. Soft lithography is applied to make micro channels and small compartments through which fluids such as blood plasma can be drawn. There are many lab-on-a-chip applications. For example, small "fingers" made sensitive to particular molecules can be exposed to fluids. When triggered, some fingers give off small electric charges, others change color or fluoresce.

The astounding thing is how easy these labs-on-a-chip are to make. Patterns are etched into silicon wafers by computer-controlled electron beams. PDMS — common silicone caulk — is poured over the etched wafer surface and fills the negative spaces. The PDMS is allowed to harden and then carefully peeled off. Intricate positive structures of soft, bio-stable PDMS remain on the underside. These tiny channels, gates, mixing rooms and wells are excellent structures for micromanipulation of fluid. Layers can be joined to make more complex fluid processing systems — labs-on-a-chip. The structures are simple but can have features down to about six nanometers—about half the Moore's law threshold in semiconductors today.[11]

Student projects typically mix or match techniques to make small systems. In our class, I planned a lab-on-a-chip using a mix of detection techniques to look in parallel for 20 micro molecules in blood. These particular molecules have been recently discovered to signal and perhaps cause — by cascade effects — positive real-time effects of aerobic exercise on the heart and pancreas. Speaking to J.D. one afternoon, I commented on the extraordinary flexibility of the bio Nano techniques, and their ability to be mixed and matched into applications. *"Yes,"* said J.D., *"it is like there are all of these components available on a table in front of us, and we just draw lines through a handful of them and out to what we want to do."[12]*

That is a perfect homolog for the strands and fabrics linking functions on a system-on-a-chip, chips in a system, people and teams in a value chain, and companies among each other in an ecosystem.

NOTES

[1] "How I Accidentally Kickstarted the Domestic Drone Boom," Chris Anderson, Wired Magazine, June 22, 2012 http://www.wired.com/dangerroom/2012/06/ff_drones/all/

[2] "Moore's law to roll on for another decade," Gordon Moore speaking to the International Solid-States Circuits Conference, IEEE, February 10, 2003, CNET, February 10, 2003 http://news.cnet.com/2100-1001-984051.html

[3] William Gibson, Wikiquote, Fresh Air, NPR (31 August 1993) {unverified}, he repeated it, prefacing it with "As I've said many times..." in "The Science in Science Fiction" on Talk of the Nation, NPR (30 November 1999, Timecode 11:55) http://en.wikiquote.org/wiki/William_Gibson

[4] "There's lots of room at the bottom," Richard Feynman, Caltech Engineering and Science, Volume 23:5, February 1960, pp 22-36. http://www.zyvex.com/nanotech/feynman.html

[5] "Population diversity and ecosystem services," Gary Luck, Gretchen Daily, Paul Ehrlich, Trends in Ecology and Evolution, Vol. 18, No. 7, July 2003 http://max2.ese.u-psud.fr/epc/conservation/PDFs/luck.pdf

[6] "Cramming more components onto integrated circuits: With unit cost falling as the number of components per circuit rises, by 1975 economics may dictate squeezing as many as 65,000 components on a single silicon chip," Gordon E. Moore, The experts look ahead (editorial section), Electronics, Volume 38, Number 8, April 19, 1965 http://download.intel.com/museum/Moores_Law/Articles-Press_Releases/Gordon_Moore_1965_Article.pdf

[7] Freescale Products, Mouser Electronics Online Catalog, April 1013 http://www.mouser.com/freescalesemiconductor/

[8] Mouser Electronics, http://www.mouser.com/freescalesemiconductor/

[9] Geoff Lees and Mario Centeno, Freescale Semiconductor, Austin, Texas, personal communication, March 2013

[10] "How I Accidentally Kickstarted the Domestic Drone Boom," Chris Anderson, Wired Magazine, June 22, 2012http://www.wired.com/dangerroom/2012/06/ff_drones/all/

[11] "Recent progress in soft lithography." J.A. Rogers, R.G. Nuzzo, February 2005, Materials Today 8 (2): 50–56. doi:10.1016/S1369-7021(05)00702-9.

[12] J.D. Deng, Laboratory of Integrated Science and Engineering, Harvard University, Cambridge, Massachusetts, personal communication, February 2013

Wrap an ecosystem around every product and service

Every product and service is also a marketplace for further products and services that enrich the opportunities customers can pursue. We provide value by selecting and recruiting these resources, categorizing, testing and certifying them. We are in a prime position to collect and publish customer feedback, continuously improving the ecosystem. When we increase the access of members to each other by making markets we increase productive exchanges. Increasing exchanges creates more value faster, and advances the whole.

•

NVIDIA, Dell, AMCC, Linaro, Xilinx

•

The leadership lesson of this chapter is simple: Go for it. We live in a time when the conditions to develop business ecosystems have never been better. At its heart, a business ecosystem is an initiative based on shared purpose, with open communication and peer-oriented relationships, where the participants share and grow together. And as a general rule, most initiatives can be made stronger with an ecosystem perspective. Partly this is a function of the global diffusion of knowledge, and the ease of connecting to others. In many cases the best resources are outside of one's own company, and/or can be better accessed in a network.

The connected community has a qualitatively new culture of collaboration — very broadly shared, cross-industry, ultra competent and with a large global population of members. This worldwide growth medium, this "yogurt culture" for business, is more or less invisible to most observers, but it is the secret sauce in the stew, the Miracle Grow in the soil.

In the following pages we will examine four distinct ecosystems that are planted in the soil of the connected community. These demonstrated four different ways to succeed. Taken together these stories also illuminate the overall benefits available in the connected community.

But the major lesson here is "go for it." This is your time. There will be successors to the connected community. But your reason to act now is that you can see this one. There are, as I'm sure you have noticed, many in tech who can't see or can't figure out how to understand the current landscape. Here is a warning: that may be us in the next era. The important features of the next era may literally be invisible to us. So make your move now, while you can see this one.

Consider a recent collaboration between NVIDIA and ARM. Phil Carmack is the head of NVIDIA's mobile business. About a year-and-a-half ago he developed an idea for improvements to the ARM Cortex-A9 processor, which NVIDIA wanted to integrate alongside an LTE cellular modem. He went to see ARM CEO Warren East in his office in Cambridge UK travelling from California where he works and lives.

> *"I drove four hours to get to Warren's office, sat in his lobby so that he would talk with me ...*

> *"'There's a theme here Warren. I think it's a great opportunity [to improve the Cortex-A9 processor design] if we could work together on this.' And he said, 'OK, Phil, we will do it.'"*

The collaboration began by examining the real feasibility of Phil's suggestion. As Phil says,

> *"If you're a participant in a market as efficient as this, you're running flat out. You don't have much time to adapt and change course. So it should be an important decision. [We needed a solid process, we just needed it fast.] Sure, I would have liked just for them to believe that NVIDIA has all the answers and whatever NVIDIA says, that's what we should do. That's not very realistic.*

> *"On the other hand, we recognized that this new design wasn't [going to make it into the next manufacturing cycle] unless we got it done really quickly, three or four months. So we managed it to be as simple as humanly possible. We both put effort in to make it work.*

> *"The result was a dramatic improvement in terms of performance per watt, while still keeping a really small [ARM processor] core area.*

> *"There was no consulting arrangement. We both did it for the good of the ecosystem. These ideas we shared freely with each other just raised the value of the ecosystem and we recognized it. In the end [NVIDIA] might be helping our competitors to a certain extent. But we are also making it possible to create a product that is kind of amazing. So we are happy*

that it turned out that way."[1]

A few things stand out in this story. First, Phil made the meeting happen quickly. Warren was open to it. The substance of Phil's visit was obviously compelling — a credit to Phil's vision. Yet what then happened would be remarkable in other organizational communities: both were willing and able to commit themselves and their organizations. Literally a few months later the chip was being baked in silicon.

An earlier chapter highlighted a similar story in which Robert Hormuth of Dell flew to Los Angeles to meet with Ian Drew. Out of that, a multi-year joint study of servers, and ultimately a project to build servers — in turn in an ecological relationship with several ARM ecosystem fabless chip companies, and their choices of fabs. Super credit to Robert for the ideas and initiative, super credit to both for the relationship-making process.[2]

During this time the ARM high performance chipmakers were emerging in a similar co-evolutionary fashion. We met Paramesh Gopi briefly in the first chapter. His company AMCC is one of four key companies working with Frank Frankovsky at Facebook on transforming the server architecture of the largest scale data centers.

> *"I left Marvell in 2008. In the summer of 2008 for about three months I spent [my time] hanging around with all the big cloud data center guys, and it was apparent that there needed to be a change relative to server architecture."*

At the time, the Intel architecture market was saturated, so it would be hard to gain a foothold.

> *"IBM PowerPC was the obvious choice, but it was a closed ecosystem.*

> *"I'd worked with Apple on the iPhone when I was at Marvell, with Jobs and the whole initial iPhone team. They control a closed ecosystem for a large, very large market."*

Paramesh had experienced the downside of a closed ecosystem, even within the success story of the iPhone.

> *"After talking to key customers in China, and the web services guys, we all said, 'You know, the PowerPC is a closed ecosystem ... IBM controls rate of resolution. IBM controls peripherals. IBM controls architecture to the point where they dictate and preside over any type of architectural input, so as to not fundamentally change their inherent closely controlled server and services.'*

"So, it became obvious that we needed to go off and think about ours, especially when [a very large Chinese customer] said, 'You know what? If you guys are going to do anything, why don't you build an ARM?'"

Paramesh wondered, could they *"understand that the performance aspect of this is going to be so critical? It's not your conventional ARM mobile core."*

So Paramesh contacted Tom Cronk, head of ARM's processor division, to explore a joint commitment to ultra-high-performance. Each side had questions: AMCC had questions about performance, and ARM had questions about whether a company the size of AMCC could pull off co-designing a new architecture.

"We spent multiple meetings at [a special location near] Hyde Park because it was a secret project."

Both sides were convinced.

"ARM wanted to make sure we wouldn't screw things up and fragment the architecture. One of the things we [jointly] decided was they would adopt our strategy of not just building a better CPU but building a better server."

In his view the result is a significant win.

Paramesh credits this as an ecosystem success.

"We've broken multiple records from a business ecosystem perspective. It's taken Intel roughly a half a billion to three-quarter billion dollars [to do a similar program]. We've done it in less than, you know, less than one-fourth that budget."[3]

This open, collaborative community manifests open source community processes in its transparency, information sharing, joint experimentation and wisdom of crowds. Sometimes the crowd is small — the joint feasibility study by ARM and AMCC comprised less than ten people from each company, as did the joint project between NVDIA and ARM — but sometimes the crowd can be quite large.

However, in contrast to the typical open source project, in these cases the open process can be wrapped in secrecy when necessary — in the AMCC story about three years — and maintain its openness at the team and inter-organizational levels.

Even more interesting is that this community is making and managing investments in which can reach into the billions. And this in turn boosts proliferation and multiplies the effect of its ideas.

Third generation ecosystems can start small. They sound puny at first — powerful later. They are subject to an excellent set of Darwinian fitness requirements: Third-generation ecosystems get off the ground in their early stages only if representatives of individual companies see enough self-interested value in the project that they are willing to participate. And the self-interested value must be calculated knowing that their competitors — participating or not — will benefit as well.

By contrast in a vertically integrated company you must convince someone up the hierarchy. In a first-generation business ecosystem you must convince an executive of a keystone company or its corporate venture arm. Neither of these fitness landscapes is even close to as rigorous as the enlightened-self-interest of your peers in third-generation partner companies.

So far we've reflected on three stories of newness at NVDIA, Dell, and AMCC. Let's now look at a different aspect of the ecosystem. We will consider another arena where one can "go for it" using a purpose-built ecosystem: Oft-times in technology there are existing problems to clean up that, when fixed, will open the way forward. This is the dreaded legacy systems problem.

When the legacy issue stems from the community spending money on duplicative and not-particularly-differentiating technology, all of the affected partners need to be involved. The point of the exercise is to get everyone using the new, common bits of technology. In general companies will not adopt something of this nature unless they helped create it.

One such initiative is Linaro, which is developing shared Linux middleware that can be used with the Android operating system on a range of devices.

George Grey is the CEO of Linaro. I met with George one morning this winter at the Main Street Café near my home in Concord, Massachusetts. My three-year-old refers to the café affectionately as "the muffin store" for the raisin bran muffins. The cafe was George's choice and is my favorite place in town. George was relaxed, cheerful in business casual. We sat atop barstools at a pine table in the back of the café.

George described the Android and Linux situation that he faced when he began working on Linaro,

> *"In Linux you had Intel that invests from top to bottom. You had all these ARM companies doing their own thing.*

"Now together it is actually a lot bigger ecosystem than Intel's. But individually none of them had clout.

"And so we went to all these companies and said, 'Look, we can't go on like this. It's costing you a lot of money. You're maintaining a lot of code. Let's all agree what the functionality is, and then we will just do it once.'

"But it is a lot harder to do this when it is after the event and everybody has their own proprietary piece of software. But so, anyway, we are getting there.

"And instead of ARM having to fund all this, which it can't afford to do, it's shared amongst all of the ARM SoC vendors.

"Now, the interesting thing here is that when you think about the value of ARM, to me, ARM's value is not in low power. I mean yes, their DNA is low power. They've come from the mobile space and therefore low power is a technology benefit for ARM. But ARM's value is much more in the business model, and the fact that it enables huge innovation and differentiation very quickly."[4]

Yes, it is a powerful model, and "ARM" has become shorthand for the system of hundreds of interpenetrating third-generation business ecosystems, thriving together in the open culture of the connected community.

Another type of ecosystem development is for a firm to create forward-facing application software for the end-customer. The conceptual model for this in the smartphone world is the Apple or Google app store. The customer is able to buy a program and download to his or her phone, or download a front-end to a cloud service. Either way the customer is — ideally — able to depend upon the quality of the app and have it "just work." Each of these applications may be said to have its own ecosystem — thus Google maps, or Evernote or Angry Birds create communities, and have others developing extensions to their software and using it as a platform

One of the challenges for a Google or an Apple is managing the vast number of applications and ecosystems that can develop on the platform. This class of problem, we will see, is not limited to the consumer app stores — as a megatrend it is coming in some form to every part of the ecosystem that touches a large number of end customers. For example, Xilinx:

Xilinx makes systems-on-a-chip that serve some very complex applications. One of their major initiatives is in smart vision. That is, taking video data and analyzing it. This means looking for patterns in ambiguous data — making sense of it, and doing something. A lot of what they do is in automotive applications, where obviously the software must make an interpretation in moments — in order to prevent a crash with another car, avoid hitting a child or keep the car on track while sliding on ice.

Xilinx has three other major thrusts in variations of smarter networks — smarter wired, wireless, and data center. In each case "smart" involves understanding moment-by-moment network conditions, including equipment performance, outages, traffic patterns, loads, applications and adjusting overall for many different dimensions of higher performance.

Xilinx has, like most companies in the connected community, amazing underlying technology. Their chips are fully programmable, meaning that the same off-the-shelf chip can power a diversity of the very complex applications mentioned above.

Their chips are built principally of FPGAs — field programmable gate arrays. These are vastly capable arrays of transistors that can be reprogrammed. The range of "identities" they can take goes from mainstream calculations and logic, to fast algorithms for vision or communications analysis, to analog to digital signal converters that are part of software defined radios. They can be programmed to connect to input and output devices from medical equipment to auto steering, and on the other side to GPS, accelerometer, chemical sensors — and on and on.

In addition to the programmable areas on a chip, other dedicated resources can be made available. Typically this would include a general-purpose processor as well as specialized accelerators tuned for particular jobs. The routing on the chip among the areas is as programmable as the logic that does the work in each area. Xilinx SoCs are little digital ecosystems. Seen from a systems perspective the microelectronics field is ecosystem after ecosystem after ecosystem, all the way down.

I spoke with Steve Glaser and Dave Tokic from Xilinx. Steve is Senior Vice President, Corporate Strategy & Marketing Group; Dave is Senior Director, Partner Ecosystems and Alliances.

Steve and Dave are on their fourth company leading ecosystem development. They have become experts at it, systematic and comprehensive. Impressive.

Steve and Dave make a pair — energetic, quick thinking and able to finish each other's sentences. Xilinx headquarters is in San Jose, on "Logic Drive" — you have to love it — on the southwest side of the city, near the foothills. Despite the building being a typical Silicon Valley 2-story "earthquake shelter" office building, Xilinx is only a couple of miles from open space. It's a pretty sweet location.

Steve started, expressing the multi-ecosystem view typical of leaders in the connected community,

> *"We're unique [the company Xilinx]. We're actually part of the ARM ecosystem in a way. We are a customer of ARM's. ARM is a customer of ours. They use our products in various ways. Then we have our own ecosystem around our platform, aspects of which involve ARM, some of which don't. Some of which complement ARM and ARM is part of the solution. Sometimes they're not. So it's actually a web of things.*

> *"We have an area we call our Smarter Vision Initiative; around image and video processing systems that are adding all this intelligence to video. Interpreting what's in video say, helping in driver assistance. Processing of video and deciding if there's a kid going across the street so that your car can automatically save the child."*

Steve became audibly energized as he talked about a hybrid ecosystem that mixes open source with commercial contributions,

> *"Obviously we have a huge vested interest to tap into these hybrid models … So we tap into open source, for example around ARM's embedded Linaro.*

> *"There's something called Open CD, for example, which is an open source library of functions that people use to build these Smarter Vision systems.*

> *"With OpenCD we even modified some things so it would automatically go into a high-speed hardware acceleration function. The customer can have it either way — use the accelerator, or simply run OpenCD on ARM cores. There can be an enhanced version of OpenCD, or a plain one.*

> *"So if someone has a special purpose that is very relevant to meeting their system requirements, they can incorporate a variety of specialized dedicated hardware."*

Steve continued, highlighting how their Smarter Vision ecosystem is composed, looking forward.

> *"We have major IP partners that invest in intellectual property — large [general purpose] subsystems, real-time video engines for example, or*

[vertical-market applications] that do something in, say, communications for security. We can't do all the IP ourselves.

"[So then partners are integrating] hardware, software, intellectual property, tools, design services 'cause we can't do all the design services. If someone wants help, you name it, we do it [within the ecosystem model]. In the case of IP, whether it's for profit, whether it's open source, whether it's a hybrid of all of that, which it often is."

I ask what keeps him up at night?

"Well, I'll let Dave jump in a minute, but I'll tell you the thing that keeps me up at night ...

"Our goal is to provide an ecosystem that complements what we do and aggregates into solutions that our customers ultimately are demanding. Now that is a challenge. Let's say that we end up with hundreds of millions of dollars of business associated with one ecosystem partner's capability. What happens if that ecosystem partner gets acquired — or goes away?

"So there's this tension [about dependence]. Our biggest customers sometimes demand that we take more direct ownership of some of these key elements. Or they ask us to back it in some way even if it's from a third party. They sometimes want us to step up and take a bigger role in terms of liability and quality assurance and integration.

"Ideally it all sounds wonderful to spur on all these complementary elements of an ecosystem that add up to all these different solutions that no one company could ever create.

"But then practically it creates at some point almost too much success. In certain areas it creates extremely difficult dilemmas in terms of business continuity and assurance — for some of our big customers and certainly for us when we start having a dependency that's too high.

"Obviously you could solve this if you have several sources and they are all equal. But often in these cases they are not all equal. There are only so many people that are really good at what they do."[5]

Dave Tokic came in.

"Ultimately Xilinx can't do everything. We're not going to vertically integrate. That's not our business, it's not our strategy

"So a key piece is having a healthy ecosystem that can supply these customer needs, and the challenge is that these tend to be pretty complex systems. And the intelligence behind them requires specialized intellectual property products, whether it's hardware or software or expert services to help augment the capabilities of the end customer that's trying to implement that system.

"It's not like Apple's app store. These guys are typically PhDs in image processing or in communication theory and there are just not 10,000 of those guys or gals out there.

"So we've evolved as a company to have a more strategic relationship with our customers and they're looking to us to provide guidance. That, in turn, requires us to have a much deeper relationship with the providers. We need to proactively get them on board our latest technologies, align roadmaps, help with quality assurance.

"So I'd say it's, it's interesting. It's not a 'spread seeds all over the field and let's just reap what is sown.' You have to be very, very picky about planting a particular seed and watering it carefully in order to get the best blooms out of that plant."[6]

Xilinx has a variety of mechanisms it is using with its third parties. They range from training, to helping fund specific technology development, to taking equity investments. In rare cases they have acquired a firm.

Steve and Dave take a population approach to the partners that make up their ecosystems. They have about 600 parties that they deal with, with about fifteen in the top tier, providing mission-critical services on programs like Smarter Vision. These are companies Dave works with very closely. Then there is a second, much larger tier, that also gets active assistance, but through a less-directly-engaged consultative and training approach.

An ecosystem, like any organization or team, requires leadership. It may have a different form from a company, but it needs shared vision, management systems from aligned roadmaps to certification and testing. Partners have staffing, training and coaching challenges. Sometimes they have business model or funding problems. Steve and Dave are continuing to expand the range of ways they can help their partners be expert and successful.

In addition to providing leadership to the ecosystem members, a second role Steve and Dave have carved out is looking for gaps in their technology, in their services, and in their partner network. The goal is to identify what they call "boulders" — substantial problems holding back customer and partners, of a magnitude that is difficult to address except with guidance and perhaps funding

44

from the Xilinx level. In this way Xilinx is operating similarly to what we have seen in earlier chapters in those working in new markets —systematically identifying customer pain and problems, and systematically putting together initiatives to solve them.

The leaders of these companies see themselves involved in many ecosystems, some broader, some deeper, all overlapping and reciprocal. "I'll be in your ecosystem if you'll be in mine." Each company has its own unique and evolving configuration, shaped in constant interaction with other companies.

It should come as no surprise that the technology world continues to come up with advances in large-scale, fast-moving cooperation. The industry is deregulated, its hiring practices are very open and diversity-friendly when compared to other fields, it is international, it has a culture that celebrates science-and-innovation, it's well funded and it creates a lot of labor-saving value and thus is highly paid by the society as a whole.

Twenty years ago observers "discovered" the growth medium that was Silicon Valley. The large, first-generation business ecosystems were established in its soil. Intel, Microsoft (a Redmond version), Oracle, Cisco, Google. Books were written about the Valley's open, cooperative business style, its speed of thought and action. Other towns, London and Singapore, Bangalore, Austin, Pittsburgh and New York, as well as San Francisco just up the bay — worked to replicate its key features, and in many ways they were successful.

Today a new growth medium, even more collaborative and open has emerged. The stunning thing about the new connected community is that it is not centered in the United States at all. It is truly global. To the extent it partakes of a regional culture of origin that would be the reserved "just enough" British scientific and academic culture. Debate is considered excellent and vigorous when it is quiet, reflective, and settled by fact and clarity of thought.

This book is an attempt to describe some of its features. The leadership lesson in this chapter, it seems to me, is that this new environment is so rich, so supportive, that it broadly makes sense to go for it in establishing ecosystems. By this I certainly don't mean to be imprudent, but I think the general advice of the leaders in this chapter is that almost any initiative that is of interest to you might be enriched by an ecosystem approach.

NOTES

[1] Phil Carmack, NVDIA, personal communication, April 2013

[2] Robert Hormuth, Dell, personal communication, April 2013

[3] Paramesh Gopi, AMCC personal communication, April 2013

[4] George Grey, Linaro, personal communication, March 2013

[5] Steve Glaser, Xilinx, personal communication, April 2013

[6] Dave Tokic, Xilinx, personal communication, April 2013

Draw deeply from science and engineering

S cience and engineering are the most fundamental inputs to innovation in a business ecosystem. University and private labs are rich sources of ideas. Bringing an idea forward requires a team of experts including those who understand the discovery and those who know the industrial situation. The typical time frame for moving a discovery out of the lab to market is a decade or more. Our business ecosystems must have at their core processes of science translation — Bell Lab's "reduction to practice" — where people can work closely, in secret, at the highest professional levels, for a decade or more. This is in fact, what does happen in our best ecosystems, an incredible feat little appreciated beyond the inner walls.

•

Synopsys, SOI Consortium, Nanoelectronics Research Initiative, College of Nanoscale Science and Engineering SUNY Albany, UC Berkeley Electrical Engineering Department

•

If you want to improve your business, find relevant fields of science and engineering and get closer to the research programs and results — read journals, trade publications and textbooks. Look for ways to incorporate the findings in your business or, better yet, get acquainted with professional researchers in the field and explore ongoing collaboration.

This, in simple form, is a leadership lesson I found at nearly every turn as I interviewed executives across the connected community. It was fascinating to realize the extent that university research contributes to the "Moore's law" process advances in fabs. The connected community and its many business ecosystems do not live in isolation. Both levels, overall community and purpose-built ecosystems tap deep, active roots in the scientific and engineering communities.

Companies across the connected community routinely access advanced science and engineering research. This may involve just a rapid dip into a topic by way of reading published papers. There are many scientific papers, for example, on power saving techniques, published by university researchers as well as companies that have a long history of working on semiconductors such as IBM and Texas Instruments.

There are also large groups and organizations dedicated to fusing the talents of companies, independent research organizations, and universities when it comes to the core science that makes industry progress possible. For deeper fusion there are multi-year programs with an ecosystem of partners. The SOI Industry Consortium has been running a program on power-saving for many years. Its ecosystem has university affiliates including University of California Berkeley(US), Stanford University(US), Centro Universitário da FEI (Brazil), Kanazawa Institute of Technology (Japan), Ritsumeikan (Japan), Universite Catholoque de Louvain (Belgium) These universities are matched with EDA companies Cadence, Mentor Graphics and Synopsys, core library and IP companies ARM, IBM and Synopsys; and foundries Freescale, GlobalFoundries, IBM and UMC.[1]

Another cooperative institution, the Semiconductor Research Corporation, bills itself as "Pioneers in Collaborative Research."[2] Over 130 universities are members, as well as an almost endless list of companies in the semiconductor industry and many members of the connected community. Its Nanoelectronics Research Initiative, started in 2005, has identified roughly 20 new technologies that may be able to supersede today's state of art technologies.

In addition, academic institutions are starting nanoscience departments to pursue issues of interest to the connected community. For example, the new State University of New York College of Nanoscale Science and Engineering, Albany[3] was started in 2004 and is part of multibillion dollar co-investment between New York State, IBM, GlobalFoundries and others. Its goal is to create an advanced research cluster, with students and employees numbering in the thousands, to study, develop, and, at fabs being built in the region, manufacture next generation devices.

Tapping into these academic departments, consortia and institutes is simple in theory. Many are open and transparent public resources. Most consortia actively seek members and are open to companies across the connected community and beyond. On the other hand, translating research to practice requires dedicated effort often over a decade or longer.

The phrase "reduction to practice" appears in US patent law and means "embodiment of the concept of an invention."[4] This term can take on a broader meaning, over the years in members of the Bell Labs staff in particular seem to have come to use it as a kind of mantra emphasizing the value and the relative difficulty of getting a good idea to work well. There is a kind of genius in reduction to practice, similar to the experimental researcher with a knack for coming up with an elegant experiment. Reduction to practice is taking a discovery — for example a small change in transistor geometry that appears to be able to save power and increase speed — and turning that discovery into something that works in the world — and not just in our minds.

FinFET is a technology that is currently contributing to progress in Moore's law. It is much in the news and is celebrated as an industry advance.

Briefly FinFET is a design approach wherein the transistors on a chip, field effect transistors ("FET"), are made with a 3D structure that has what can be loosely called a "fin." The finned transistors leak less electricity and run faster that flat "planar" transistors.

Now, to whom should we credit FinFET? We can thank academic research and the same US government agency that brought us the Internet: the Defense Advanced Research Projects Agency (DARPA).

> *"FinFETs have their technology roots in the 1990s, when DARPA looked to fund research into possible successors to the planar transistor. A UC Berkeley team led by Dr. Chenming Hu proposed a new structure for the transistor that would reduce leakage current."[5]*

In order to facilitate the reduction to practice of FinFET, Chenming Hu himself became Chief Technology Officer of the Taiwan Semiconductor Manufacturing Company from 2001 to 2004.[6]

> *"Leading foundries estimate the additional processing cost of 3D devices to be 2% to 5% higher than that of the corresponding Planar wafer fabrication. FinFETs are estimated to be up to 37% faster while using less than half the dynamic power or cut static leakage current by as much as 90%."[7]*

In a tech world obsessed with power saving, battery life, and the massive electrical demands of cloud computing, FinFET is a no brainer. FinFET is just one of many advances drawn from scientific and engineering work done in academic or independent research centers. For the connected community, these discoveries are accessible and can form seeds of new commercial technologies once they are reduced to practice.

I had a set of particularly enlightening conversations with Phil Dworsky and Rich Goldman at electronic design automation company Synopsys. In order to implement FinFET, Synopsys partnered with foundry TSMC, the Berkeley research group founded by Chenming Hu and colleagues, and ARM research and development professionals. Rich gave me a sense of what the reduction to practice required:

*"There is no way forward without collaboration, at least with us in our
industry. And not only is it collaboration between two companies, but it's
collaboration between three or more companies, and they all have to
come together.*

*"For example, to implement FinFET at TSMC we [Synopsys] worked
closely with ARM very early. We all have to work together very early on to
prove that it can work. Then once you get to that point that you're able to
make something that works, you then have to work together to develop a
[design tool methodology] that the end user to can use to do the same
thing."*

In addition to making a process work, the success of an electronic design
automation tool company — like Rich's company Synopsys — has to be on two
sides. It has to work in the fab, in light and silicon and electricity — and it has to
work for design engineers who want to spec out a final chip, push a button, and
have their chip in hand not long after.

As Rich says, you have to have design tools that make the end user, the design
engineer, efficient and successful.

*"If you can't deliver effective tools then all that work has been for naught.
To deliver that requires, again, an additional period of close collaboration
with at least three parties, and probably even a fourth party, which is the
lead customer."[8]*

Phil Dworsky, Rich's colleague at Synopsys, came in at this point to describe
making the tools, which involves creating models of the light and physics of the
specific processes being used, models that address a specific chip architecture
and layout, and models to guide the machines that will do the manufacturing.
Layout requires respecting design rules for managing issues such as heat,
radio-frequency interference, or the "quantum-tunneling" problem that is a
leading cause of power loss. Phil added,

*"Absolutely all of these collaborations require multiple years. Just going
from conventional design to a well-known fabrication process using
proven design tools can take five years from idea to volume production."*

Now factor in new ideas for new processes having new design rules and
requiring new types of design software.

*"It requires a process of understanding and modeling, experimentation,
multi-way tuning and optimization — there is just an awful lot that goes
into making that happen. Then finally we get it into the advanced*

designers' hands – and they're starting to do their pilot projects. Then we get into early production and then finally we get into mainstream. If we look at the lower power work we did — together with ARM – it took about seven years."[9]

The major lesson of this chapter is to draw deeply from advances in science and engineering. The lesson of these cases for the connected community is that it is a long-term, patient and demanding process—but one that is essential to the advances of the community. Without that science and engineering input, the whole community stagnates.

Drawing deeply requires cooperative teams that can stay together for years, and do so with very open, cross-company sharing among themselves, while maintaining secrecy toward the outside world—sometimes among the companies of the members themselves.

There is an important additional leadership lesson as well: The human side of this process requires intellectual and emotional intelligence — what Phil called in this context "maturity."

"The attributes [our team members need] are maturity and a sense of what's needed, because it's almost like living in another foreign language. You need to be able to translate it always in terms of someone else's objectives and be able to demonstrate to one person what the other needs and, and why that makes sense for both to do that."[10]

Rich and Phil spoke of the management systems required, starting with respect for all members of the collaborative team — scientists, engineers from the foundry, software tool and IP, and device side — combined with the need to maintain silence and secrecy about the content of the work. Often the mere fact that a particular company is considering a new fabrication is a competitive secret.

Choices frequently have consequences that affect members of the cross-company team differently. As Phil put it, the team's job is to find solutions that both work and "create the most area under the curve" of positive results for all involved.

"… we basically have to strive to convince others, even internal to our company of the righteousness of a certain project. We need to create the business case that faces all directions."

Phil makes much of the benefits of 360 degree business cases. Carefully written out cases help each representative articulate what is important to that person's company, how it can be measured, and what the representative and company might trade off to achieve higher priorities. By making these cases available to all, other members become skilled over time at understanding each others' positions when collectively evaluating a choice. As Rich stated the overall goal:

> *"Our job is to understand the others' challenges and be able to translate between them, because we're trying to pull together multiple parties within and outside of the company along a solutions path that requires each to give and take. It's a negotiation on all sides.*
>
> *"The other side of this is to realize just how pragmatic and practical the whole electronics industry is. We all take what we can get and then we have got to solve the problem somehow. Those who have been exposed to all sides have the understanding that things are sometimes imperfect and you have to adapt, move and change to facilitate more productivity. EDA is all about productivity, making sure that our customers can take what we give them and use it on this really difficult challenge to quickly and reliably get to a result."[11]*

All across the connected community people are taking ideas — game changing ideas in many instances — and carrying on the down-at-the-workbench tasks of reducing them to practice. In this chapter I hope to have highlighted those who dip into advanced science and engineering and how much they mean to the connected community and the ecosystems within it. With the specialized and open-to-all business models of the connected community the advances made possible in reduction to practice become widely available. Thus the benefit of this work is leveraged many times over. Tapping into advances in science and engineering proliferates through and very much serves the connected community, the ecosystems, and the customers.

NOTES

[1] SOI Industry Association, Ecosystem, http://www.soiconsortium.org/about-soi/ecosystem.php

[2] Nanoelectronics Research Initiative, Semiconductor Research Corporation
http://www.src.org/program/nri/

[3] State University of New York at Albany, - College of Nanoscale Science and Engineering,
http://cnse.albany.edu/PioneeringAcademics/Constellations/Nanoengineering.aspx

[4] United States Patent and Trademark Office, Manual of Patent Examining Procedure, 2138.05
"Reduction to Practice"

[5] "FinFET: The Promises and the Challenges, Synopsys Insight Newsletter, Issue 3, 2012
http://www.synopsys.com/COMPANY/PUBLICATIONS/SYNOPSYSINSIGHT/Pages/Art2-finfet-
challenges-ip-IssQ3-12.aspx

[6] Chenming Hu, University of California at Berkeley,
http://www.eecs.berkeley.edu/Faculty/Homepages/hu.html

[7] "FinFET: The Promises and the Challenges, Synopsys Insight Newsletter, Issue 3, 2012
http://www.synopsys.com/COMPANY/PUBLICATIONS/SYNOPSYSINSIGHT/Pages/Art2-finfet-
challenges-ip-IssQ3-12.aspx

[8] Rich Goldman, Vice President, Corporate Marketing & Strategic Alliances, Synopsys, personal
communication, April 2013

[9] Phil Dworsky, Director, Strategic Alliances & Publisher of Synopsys Press, Synopsys, personal
communication, March, April 2013

[10] Ibid.

[11] Rich Goldman, Vice President, Corporate Marketing & Strategic Alliances, Synopsys, personal
communication, April 2013

Take just enough

Greed spoils business ecosystems. Open ecosystems are gift economies that depend on reciprocal care. They require considering a situation from all sides. Get clear on a fundamental choice: you can grow your business by growing the ecosystem and advancing the opportunities for your customer. You can also grow a business — at least in terms of revenues and profits — by taking from your ecosystem and from your customers. The philosophy of "just enough" is not about austerity. Indeed, those in the connected community are thriving. It is about caring for your partners, not "sucking the life out of them" by exerting your bargaining power when they are weaker. It is about gaining your security and your enjoyment and your accomplishments with others — in ways that are sustainable as a business, an organization and a person.

•

Mentor Graphics, ARM Holdings

•

Some years ago Laura Nash and Howard Stevenson wrote a fine and provocative book called *Just Enough*.[1] Laura teaches ethics at Harvard Business School and Howard founded and led the school's program for entrepreneurs. On the basis of observing the careers of former students over many decades, they concluded that the happiest are those who pursue "just enough" personal achievement, and then allow themselves to be interdependent with communities and families who enjoy and nurture them. A "just enough" approach recognizes that individuals inescapably live in community, and that the natural course of a sustainable life is for a person to contribute to the community, and for the community in all its diversity and richness and care to help that person develop their gifts and live a good life.

The ecosystem-level business model of the connected community is precisely "just enough," substituting companies for individuals, and the ecosystem for family and community. Wally Rhines, CEO of Mentor Graphics, was one of the earliest leaders in the connected community, signing the second ARM license, after LSI Logic, in 1992 while at Texas Instruments. When he moved to Mentor Graphics he continued to be a partner. He described how he and his colleagues gradually began to realize the full benefits of the ecosystem model:

"There were economies of scale associated with the ecosystem design that we didn't recognize at the time, but became very important. We did recognize the importance of an embedded software infrastructure and third party contributions.

"Supporting an architecture requires enormous resources. Resources in design and verification and software development and support applications. And really there haven't been that many prolific architectures just because the amount of work is so large, and no one company can do it.

"The economies of scale came in having one company do it and a lot of other companies using it as a building block for creating more value in their particular design — where they put a lot of additional logic around it and targeted it at specific market segments."

"As a leader, is there a lesson in all this?" I asked. After a moment he replied,

"The first thing is to keep an open mind about contributions from other people and to be very parsimonious with your own time and resources so that you spend your time doing what you do best."

"Is there a life lesson that you might want to pass on to your children regarding this topic?" I asked.

"The life lesson for my children is work at something that's really interesting and changing and evolving because it'll attract other interesting people. They will do other interesting things and create opportunities and excitement for you in your life."[2]

"Just enough" yields "lots more."

In business as in life there are things one does well, and things one doesn't. The theory is simple: with each party giving its best, the ecosystem as a whole gives its collective best.

While it is clear that this model is good for the whole if it can be maintained, an observer would ask what keeps stronger companies from preying on the weak? What keeps companies from consolidating key industry services like electronic design automation and denying them to others?

The answer is that leaders of the ecosystem are proactively shaping an ethos that encourages "just enough" restraint across the ecosystem, in the name of enabling closer collaboration, deeper specialization, and growing the whole. Given a choice of growing a company alone, or growing an industry and an ecosystem, these leaders understand that they are linked, and they must do all three.

A "just enough" lifestyle is attractive to others in both business ecosystems and in community life. It helps recruit talent and companies into the ecosystem, eases entry into new markets, builds customer trust and gives companies the security to more deeply collaborate.

In other ecosystems there is much talk of "lock-in" — of forced dependency. In the ARM ecosystem the relationships are closer than I've experienced in any comparable ecosystem, but people talk of interdependence and community. One day it struck me, the term "lock-in" arises when there is a fundamental break in the business relationship. Otherwise the experience and the term is intimacy.

I had a recent discussion with Simon Segars on "just enough." Simon was employee number 16 at ARM, and will become CEO of the company on July 1st. He was quite clear on ARM's partner-favorable policies. I asked if he felt ARM was leaving money on the table and he said,

> *"Well yes, that's a common question we get from investors, though lately less so. Maybe that is because we've been having the conversation for so long about it.*
>
> *"Investors will sometimes say, 'You're so, you know, strongly penetrated in a particular market segment. What stops you from multiplying your royalties by ten?'*
>
> *"So a great example of why we don't do that is because we do want to see our technology deployed as broadly as possible and if we were egregious in our royalties because of the strength of our market, we wouldn't have our customers taking us with them to other markets.*
>
> *"So this pricing and relationship making has been a very strategic thing.*
>
> *"In the '90s GSM [wireless telephony standard adopted Europe-wide] was making fast headway, and was associated with enormous markets. This market could [in principle] be served by many people like us, and many*

people wanted to get in. In our case our current customers had used our technology in many cases successfully, their engineers knew how to use the processes and they had good relationships with the company. So when they looked at this new opportunity, it was an easy decision to choose ARM."

Simon's philosophy is that the ecosystem point of view is much more than just pricing, and that members of the ecosystem have a comprehensive strategy for taking care of others across it.

"We do value partnership as a core culture in ARM. We work hard to be favorable to our partners and you know even though there are only 2,500 people in the company, spreading this philosophy across everyone sometimes gets hard.

 "We do treat our partners equally. We do really try and play nice and we really try to build an ecosystem that is self-funded. It's been very important to us that our ecosystem partners can build profitable businesses of their own, and that we're not just extracting all of their profits into our P&L."[3]

Simon used the polite term "extracting," but across my interviewees the more common phrase would be "suck the profits out of the ecosystem" and the topic was top of mind for tech leaders. The phenomenon is well discussed by Marco Iansiti in his book *The Keystone Advantage.*[4] He emphasizes that it is very difficult for a strong ecosystem player to resist investor and other pressures to take profits away from others. Essentially they do this by extorting high prices for their products —which are essential and unique — leaving little available profit for others. The weaker have little choice once they are woven into the ecosystem — their revenues, which may be large — can't be maintained if they try to get out. And the consequence is that the weaker players cease to innovate, and potential joiners to the ecosystem are scared away.

This is the narrative every single interviewee applied to the personal computer ecosystem today, noting that even though the PC ecosystem is declining, two companies continue to extract billions in earnings, and in the case of the other companies — mainly computer OEMs and ODMs — most are either just above breakeven or losing billions per year.

The connected community is designed to prevent this sort of behavior, and spread wealth around. Three realities keep the ecosystem on track. First, there is competition in the ecosystem in the vast majority of niches that keeps prices disciplined. And in the case of places where, by necessity, the ecosystem needs one standard and one steward — as in the microprocessor design — there are rivals that could be turned to if necessary. Every space in the segment is "contestable." Players are motivated to be pro-community, or the community can replace them.

Second, powerful players use creative financial terms designed to shift risk and immediate costs to the larger, stronger members — thus enabling weaker players to contain their costs so that they have their best opportunity to succeed in the marketplace.

The mechanisms are varied and inventive, and throughout they demonstrate a nuanced effort at balancing value in the ecosystem. These mechanisms are very different from the alignment-gaining payments made from monopoly players to others in first-generation ecosystems. In general the first generation payments distort payee behavior, reduce differentiation, and dampen market signals from the customer edge of the ecosystem.

In this third generation ecosystem, the mechanisms are designed to assist all of the weaker partners, without picking winners, to reduce their financial risks and costs in order to explore differentiated approaches to the market. The goal is to have many partners listen-to and amplify market signals — and let as many as possible thrive.

As I went through my study I was presented with a variety of mechanisms. Wally Rhine pointed out that semiconductor manufacturers have long practiced "forward pricing" where customers can buy a chip for what it will cost in the X millionth unit. The strong manufacturer reduces the cost of a component, reducing how much its downstream customer needs to lay aside for chips, which lets cost and price reductions cascade down through the chain end customers, and when successful helps stimulate the market.

Frank Frankovsky of Facebook shared the information that he and other cloud services companies are looking upstream to server and network equipment companies, and offering to assure a future market if vendors work together on innovations of particular value to the services companies. A similar initiative among communications carriers is called SDN, software defined network. The carriers have come together to work with their suppliers.

ARM's business model is based on tiny royalties paid when a chip is sold. A customer of ARM's pays a license and a royalty. The one-time fee for a perpetual license for a processor design is priced on a sliding scale in order to be accessible to all. Later, sometimes years later, when the licensee actually sells chips to its customers, it pays a small royalty per unit. This second part of the agreement is a gain-sharing approach, and incentivizes ARM to help the customer be successful, for example providing extensive free consulting — because of course that is the only way it will get paid royalties.

Finally, powerful companies sometimes do seem to squeeze the others in the ecosystem, or at least shift burdens to them. This can cause consternation. The principle foundry TSMC, until recently, charged its customers only for actual working chips, and TSMC absorbed the cost of defective chips. Recently TSMC began charging for chips that come off the line, putting the customer at risk in case of poor manufacturing yields. As time goes on it will be interesting to follow the response of the community to this move, which has special significance as TSMC moves to the advanced 14nm and below process nodes, where yields may be increasingly unpredictable.

What we see overall across the ecosystem is a leadership philosophy and practice designed to enable partners to focus on their special competences, work closely with others, listen to the market and customer, differentiate in the ways they think best, contribute to the community as a whole, and reap fair gains when successful.

By not exerting their market power against each other, and by employing well-designed gain sharing, this open ecosystem keeps average selling prices low and differentiation high. This makes solutions available to the largest number of people, accelerates penetration of the market and improves the lives of more customers sooner. The point of the ecosystem is to transform the world, one customer and product at a time and to do so at a rate faster than comparable systems.

NOTES

[1] Just Enough: Tools for Creating Success in Your Work and Life, Laura Nash, Howard Stevenson, Wiley, 2004

[2] Wally Rhines, Mentor Graphics, personal communication, April 2013

[3] Simon Segars, ARM Holdings, personal communication, April 2013

[4] The Keystone Advantage: What the New Dynamics of Business Ecosystems Mean for Strategy, Innovation, and Sustainability, Marco Iansiti, Roy Levien, Harvard Business Review Press, 2004

Open it

The human, technical and economic benefits of open ecosystems and the connected community are so dramatic that it seems nothing can stop them. On the other hand, a problem internal to the community itself might be posed by the actions of a rogue operator — for example a patent troll or hostile takeover opportunist. In an open, connected economy, the role of senior leaders includes being alert for challenges to the integrity of the community and leading preemptive, corrective or defensive action as necessary. Overall, the connected community and its ecosystems are growing, scaling and differentiating as organizations. This provides an opportunity for new forms of co-leadership across the community.

•

Cadence, ARM Holdings

•

There are at least two places from which a challenge to openness in the connected community and its ecosystems might arise.

The first could come from within the general body of membership, by any one of a large number of players who might decide to maximize its short-term gain at the expense of others.

The second could come from one of the large, wealthy firms in the community, who might decide to acquire or "roll up" others and consolidate a central portion of the value chain under their control. This can be a cheap way to grow short-term revenues, but over time this strategy will reduce the diversity of the value chain and ecosystems where it is used — thus weakening the whole.

A third challenge — not to openness but to overall strategic understanding — is emerging as the connected community reaches toward new levels of global scale.

Threats to openness from members within the connected community

Last year leaders in several companies noticed that well-known activist investors were joining the board of the struggling MIPS Technologies, a microprocessor design company with a number of important patents. A group

61

of companies across the community, most not publicly identified, came together and bought the core of the MIPS patent portfolio, putting it firmly in hands friendly to open ecosystems and effectively making it a public resource.[1]

In another case, a company began acquiring companies in a manner that raised concern among its closest trading partners. Their concern was that the company would achieve a controlling position in a key element of technology, become a single source, and attempt to extract higher than appropriate prices. In this case the trading partners helped a second company get established. They provided themselves a second source and ensured constructive competition.

I learned of at least one case where a company spurned a long-time supplier to start a business to supply itself — and to take products to market against its ally. Leaders of the aggrieved company confronted their former customer and argued that this action betrayed their trust. Though the former customer did not reverse itself, it is thought by observers that the resulting conflict and bad feelings served as an object lesson for all and dampened such behavior from that time forward.

These three stories demonstrate community self-regulation. They also show the difficulty of knowing when one has crossed the line, and how exactly to translate the high principles of the community into concrete business leadership. The league-level challenges of major league sports illustrate the difficulty. Consider the conflicting economics of small and large-market teams, and the near-constant tweaking of cross-subsidies, salary caps, luxury taxes and similar mechanisms in order to bring members together in the interest of the whole.

The global open connected technology community is much more complex — and yet it is functioning. Members do sacrifice for the good of the whole. How is this possible?

In the past decade, social psychology, game theory and evolutionary mathematics have shed new light on this question. Mathematical biologist Martin Nowak in his book Supercooperators discusses two sets of relevant findings.[2]

First, in what may be an example of academics verifying the obvious, research confirms that non-cooperators will turn themselves into cooperators if the probability of payoff for cooperation is high enough. In a monopoly-centered ecosystem one or a few players "take most." In an open connected community a large number of participants can anticipate success and thus will be motivated to cooperate.

- In the connected community the probability of a reasonable payoff for cooperation is quite high because among other things your partners in the community want you to succeed and will look for ways to help you.

- The extensive use of profit sharing and risk-sharing financial models, combined with "just enough" on the part of those with the strongest bargaining power, makes for a comparatively equitable distribution of gains.

- The degree of specialization in the ecosystem, combined with its enormous number of members, products and markets, means potential scale economies are great.

- The growth of the ecosystem combined with the diversity of its offerings and end markets provides a continually expanding pie. While the growth phase may not last forever, the markets being tapped are vast and many are barely touched — the growth phase in some respects may be just beginning.

- Companies are encouraged to differentiate themselves, which means their leaders and people are doing what they believe in, not what they are compelled to do. This improves recruitment and motivation, which in turn encourages people to cooperate rather than defect — because to defect would be to step away from your own self-chosen path.

Second, here is a less obvious finding from research, this time from game theory. Simulations demonstrate that when cooperation breaks down, it is more easily restored when partners have fewer neighbors. Why is this? Cooperation benefits are based on the ratio of cooperative to uncooperative neighbors. Uncooperative neighbors extract a cost against performance and cooperators augment performance.

Other factors being equal, cooperation in a hostile world can best begin from small clusters where a few partners can feed into each other's success and collectively demonstrate obvious benefits to neighbors — and entice neighbors, one or two at a time, to join and grow the cluster. If a member has only two or three immediate neighbors, that original cluster is comparatively easy to muster. If a member has ten immediate neighbors, it is difficult to put together a high percentage of cooperative neighbors, and thus almost impossible to show a cooperative benefit of interest to any other.

Why is this effect significant in the connected community? Its ecosystems are diverse and are settled into niches. Within those niches many of its most intense cooperative relationships are with small triangles of players — device maker, fab, EDA and IP and core vendors. To have success only takes a group

63

working in a small focused ecosystem and achieving a shared breakthrough. And there are many such ecosystems, in many niches.

Threats from large, wealthy firms to maintaining openness and independence in the community

Warren East is the outgoing CEO of ARM. He is deeply involved in the community and philosophical about why it works. We discussed my impressions of the high level of openness in the ARM organizational culture, and the quiet, modest confidence of so many of the people.

> *"Pleased to hear you say that. Hopefully that is the type of culture we have at ARM. I think it is a practical way of running this business that is dependent on the ecosystem. We're probably outwardly a lot less paranoid than some other companies that have a reputation for paranoia.*
>
> *"Internally, I assure you we absolutely are paranoid. And absolutely not content I would say."*

He went on to talk about the partnership business model that has ARM dependent on the success of its licensees in order to make money. He pointed out that,

> *"We are competing with different architectures and we continue to complete with multiple architectures. And our number one competitor is much, much larger scale. So, you know, there's a natural paranoia there."[3]*

Listening to Warren, it became clear to me that he, and other leaders across the community, may or may not be paranoid (I don't particularly like the phrase) — but if they are, they're paranoid about different things than those in the first-generation business ecosystems.

Strategy and business development in a traditional monopoly are about looking for companies to acquire and combine into centers of one's own monopoly power.

In the connected economy, by contrast, you might take action to help a company stay independent, thus diversifying the evolutionary pathways available to the ecosystem as a whole. You could call this "open business development." It makes little sense if your goal is to collect profits and grow your business in relative isolation from others or to their detriment. On the other hand, open business development can make great sense if you want to live in a diverse ecosystem that will transform society and proliferate technology's benefits.

The contrast is seen in the following chart of contrasting approaches to typical business ecosystem situations. In the middle column we see a first-generation, closed monopoly approach to typical business ecosystem challenges. Keystone monopolists roll up weaker players, use cash to buy loyalty, and can be single-minded in their definition of progress and innovation.

In the right hand column we see the contrast. Keystones in open ecosystems promote the benefits of diversity and independence and the flexibility born of combinations. They see possible defections as symptoms of possible ecosystem weakness and requiring shoring up. And they find it easy to rally combinations around industry-wide challenges, because innovation in the community is happening in most of the players, in a diversity of directions. The ecosystem as a whole is not dependent upon one or two players to make advances that carry the rest — and also hold the others back.

Closed and Open Business Development

Problem	First-generation monopoly	Third-generation community
The largest companies have the financial might to buy control of smaller players in key roles Yet in many cases the independence of players of all sizes and their willingness to trade broadly is vital to the connected community and its ecosystems	If you see a weak player in a critical role is struggling, buy it before one of your rivals buys it first. More aggressively, see any given domain or sphere of influence that has lots of small players as ripe for "rolling up" into a central monopoly position.	Help larger players benefit — along with the ecosystems and the connected community as a whole — by having a diversity of independent members who combine and recombine to create solutions for an ever-expanding range of problems and markets. Discourage roll-ups. Help smaller players fend off suitors if necessary. If necessary play white knight to assure vital companies or resources stay independent and open. E.g. the connected community bought the MIPS patent portfolio to keep it open for the community.
There is a large player who can afford to make its own processors and is leaning toward leaving the community.	If you are the maker of the processor (or any similar central building block, such as a software operating system, use your monopoly profits to buy loyalty where you need it. In the case of a large player considering leaving, estimate the direct cost of the defection, as well as the indirect costs it the movement spreads. Then step up and find a way to pay through for example special discounts, sales incentive payments, equity investments or loans.	Improve community services continuously. If a player is wavering it sends a strong signal that it doesn't feel able to succeed with these services. Apparently software tools, applications and developer communities are well not perceived to be ahead of alternative communities in capabilities. Where the connected community seems fragmented or weak, take shared action to build new open capability.
There are large, difficult problems facing the technology community across products and markets. Feature size, integration, mass production and cost-reduction — Moore's law — is a first-generation problem. Others include design automation and flexibility, energy efficiency and security.	In order not to be diverted from one's current roadmap, and in order to preserve one's lead, it is important for the monopoly to find a way to address new challenges within the framework of its existing investments. E.g. in the 90s traditional communications carriers attempted to put intelligence in their switched networks to counter distributed computing. They would have been better off learning computing without the baggage of integrating with their network—or concentrating on upgrading to digital networks and thus hastening the day of cloud computing.	The connected community and its ecosystems anticipate and take cooperative action to address the largest emerging issues their spheres of influence. Warren East: *"If we are to realize the promise of the digital world, and we want to have the things we are making continue to be useful to humanity, then I think security is the new energy."*

The connected community scales up

The ultimate scale of the community will be much larger than today's collection of ecosystems, which are already shipping billions of units each year. Profound economies of scale and cumulative learning will be available to large, well-funded companies who can make the requisite investments and assemble the necessary expertise. At the other end of the range, communities of small, agile players using tiny, inexpensive chips are entering markets. Leaders of the connected community are already working together to co-evolve and co-lead the next generation of ecosystems and systems of ecosystems.

Charles Huang is a senior executive at Cadence, the electronic design automation company. He is a gracious man with a philosophical turn, and we enjoyed talking about the longer view of the scene.[4]

The first observation he made was of the delight and surprise that he and others in the tech industry are experiencing at the success of the connected community and its many constituent ecosystems and companies.

> *"You know, for many years [we have been wondering who would bring the next wave] and, unbeknownst to us, it is really fun for it to be something so surprising. You can look back now. You can see how these little, little actors, without any [traditional top-down] coherent, coordinated industry policies, could provide a private free market where they gathered together to cause so much change!"*

In addition to his delight at what small companies can do together, he is paying a great deal of attention to the relationship of the ecosystems and community to the much larger actors: the telecom carriers, whose revenues and earnings are more than double those of the equipment and device makers, and a company he considers unique on the landscape, Samsung.

Samsung is of course a citizen of the connected community, and one of its largest chipmakers and chip users. Currently in the tech community, Samsung is being held up as a model of vertical integration in the traditional sense of an integrated value chain with one owner and a competitive advantage derived principally from each link trading with the others. Given this conventional wisdom, there is conversation about how far Samsung might go in the direction of what is seen as internal sourcing. This in turn is seen as a potential challenge to the ecosystem model and the connected economy.

Charles has a very different interpretation. He has close knowledge of Samsung and does not see it as having a conventional vertical integration mindset. On the contrary, in Samsung Charles sees a company that has developed a way to succeed based on capital investment.

Samsung looks vertically integrated today because it has massive positions in major parts of the information and communications technology value chain, and these units sell to each other. However, it did not get to these positions through integration and captive internal customer/supplier relations, but by more or less one-by-one picking off already commoditized markets — for example DRAM memories. Samsung also leveraged capital and R&D to lower cost so far below the industry standard as to make a profit and drive others out. As Charles says,

> *"They crushed everyone in DRAM, crushed everybody in TV, crushed everybody in flash. It has done this same thing with LCDs and with semiconductors."*

As Charles points out, Samsung's centers of excellence trade with many other companies — for example, Samsung sells screens to Sony. Samsung has until recently been Apple's biggest maker of processor chips. It would be as if each part of General Motors, or of Intel, began selling its partial products on the open market. The advantage from a scale standpoint is that volume is not solely dependent on the rest of one's company. From a learning standpoint, each part competes for outside sales on the open market against everything else available. To this last point, it is rumored that not only does Samsung sell on the open market, but it quietly buys as well — thus providing Samsung-based competition for other Samsung units.

A question Charles would like to understand: How is it that Samsung can affordably source as much capital as it does? And equally, how is it that Samsung manages the execution of its investments? Charles observes that Samsung seems refreshingly unbound by tradition or ideology in its investments, and looks for ideas and supply outside as well as in. For example, Samsung goes outside for designs and intellectual property, whether for processor designs (ARM), or whole chips (Qualcomm).

Charles does not claim at all to know Samsung's strategic mindset or future strategies. However, from my perspective, the picture Charles paints is one of a player that is principally concerned with establishing world-serving centers that provide the high-capital-investment-requiring hard components the community needs to continue to grow while reducing its total costs and selling points. From this perspective, Samsung's actions are consistent with a very helpful community member pursuing its role in an open ecosystem.

From a conventional perspective, one might see a company like Samsung as setting up these centers so it can subsequently wrap "high value" — meaning high margin — intellectual property businesses around them. That perspective makes sense if one sees the capital-requiring businesses as unattractive, and sees the volatile and fast-moving ecologies grown on top of them as more desirable. This is first-generation analysis — what it ignores is the dramatic differences between the two classes of businesses, and the very real and attractive opportunities in capital-intensive businesses if one is able to lead, learn and continually advance them. The agile, fast-moving businesses are much better suited to diverse, co-evolving communities that sit in hundreds of large, medium and niche markets, close to applications and customers.

Far from being concerned about the Samsungs of the world, the best thing the community can do for itself, as well as both large and small members, is to just keep co-evolving.

Next telecom

The telecom carriers' global mobile revenue in 2012 totaled more than a trillion dollars: $1,252,000,000,000 according to a recent MIT Technology Review report. By contrast, mobile phones and smartphones came in at $269,000,000,000, or less than a quarter of the carriers' revenues. Personal computer sales were $248,000,000,000, or twenty billion less than phones, and declining.[5]

Charles noted that until recently the differentiation maintained by phone makers was tied to their network partners. The leading device makers had the best relationships with telcos — from the executive suite to testing and certification of new models. This was consistent with carrier dominance.

But now the app world, the continued expansion of the "smart" part of the smartphone, and the use of the smartphone as a digital hub — for financial transactions, entertainment, and management of connected devices — may be changing the game. Charles observes with interest that device makers seem to be exploring ways to differentiate on the chip itself.

> *"Seeing that these cell phone device makers like Samsung, ZTE, HTC, Lenovo are now endeavoring to make their own SoCs, I would venture to guess that they now see value or differentiation shifting to the device."*

This is good for the electronic design automation and physical IP parts of the community, as these phone makers ramp up their design capabilities and engage third-party design houses.

What seems to be happening is a new round of device innovation spinning free from the carriers. The concern about Samsung — with which I disagree — was that it would use its centers of capital-intensive businesses to take over the soft goods wrapped around them. But the evidence goes against that supposed trend. The traditional carriers started out integrated in this fashion, from consumer phones to PBX systems. The traditional carriers show a decades-long devolution as their control over peripheral devices and applications sharply and steadily declines. From my perspective, these later businesses require an agility and co-evolutionary dancing that is very different from building and managing networks.

Another emerging phenomenon that may also be contributing to the devolution of carrier control is the rise of ultra-low-cost smartphones, some with a retail cost as low as $65 in China. How are these produced at this price point? MediaTek and Spreadstrum are now selling what one might call "Smartphones on a chip" — turnkey phone kits costing in the tens of dollars that are being assembled and sold by several hundred mostly small and emerging companies in China.[6]

The cheap smartphones are a topic I hear a lot about because they feel like potential disruptors to some industry leaders that benefit greatly from the current $600 smartphones. I don't know how some of the chip and assembly players participate in the new world. It does occur to me that anyone considering entering Africa or India with an inexpensive phone should be assessing these low-cost options. It also seems these phones have a real role to play in the community, and foreshadow a next round of proliferation of community technology and transformation of the world.

In closing, here is the good news: The greatest disruptive technology on the landscape today is not a product or a service, but a philosophy and a set of business practices. This system of third-generation business ecosystems, evolving together in the growth medium of the connected community, has strength and momentum. Talented people and companies are attracted to its fun, educational benefits, reasonable ecosystem-wide profit-sharing business models, and the opportunity for many to succeed.

Leaders in the connected community are self-conscious leaders who understand they are together inventing a new approach to industry. They are studying business evolution, monopoly economics (especially the downside of monopolies), and ideas of cooperation taken from game theory, social psychology and the open-source community. The words of the day are open ecosystems, collaboration, proliferation and differentiation. And so far the growth is happening, companies are succeeding, and people are happy. Not a bad start.

NOTES

[1] "Imagination Buys MIPS, While ARM Gets Access To Patents," Peter Judge, TechWeekEurope November 7, 2012 http://www.techweekeurope.co.uk/news/arm-mips-patents-imagination-98506

[2] Supercooperators, Martin A. Nowak, Free Press, 2011

[3] Warren East, ARM Holdings, personal communication, November 2012

[4] Charles Huang, Cadence, personal communication, April 2013

[5] "Smartphones: High Prices, Huge Market," Benedict Evans, MIT Technology Review Business Report — Making Money in Mobile, 2013

[6] "Here's Where They Make China's Cheap Smartphones," Case Studies, MIT Technology Review Business Report — Making Money in Mobile, 2013

I Thou

Emotional intelligence is perhaps the most important attribute of effective members of an open business ecosystem. Professional expertise matters a great deal, but if not expressed with maturity and care, the close relationships on which the ecosystem depends cannot function. Human resources strategies can be designed to recruit, train, motivate and promote those with emotional intelligence. The Jewish philosopher Martin Buber presented this idea well. He said we can treat each other and ourselves as an "it" — as objects to be driven, threatened, used. Or we can treat each other as "thou" — persons to be respected, cared for, learned from, with values, creativity and giftedness.

•

MIT, ARM Holdings

•

> *"Social networks...transport all kinds of things from one person to another. One fundamental determinant of flow is the tendency of human beings to influence and copy one another. People typically have many direct ties to a wide variety of people. And each and every one of these ties offers opportunities to influence and be influenced. Students with studious roommates become more studious. Diners sitting next to heavy eaters eat more food. And this simple tendency for one person to influence another has tremendous consequences when we look beyond our immediate connections."[1]*

In 2008 and again in 2010 Nicholas Christakis of Harvard Medical School and James Fowler of the University of California at San Diego published groundbreaking research. Using data from the Framingham Heart Study as well as other research,[2] they demonstrated that mood is contagious across social networks. As described by mathematical biologist and game theorist Martin Nowak,

> *"Happy people tend to be clustered together, not because they gravitate toward smiling people, but because of the way happiness spreads through social contacts over time."[3]*

As I got to know more leaders across the connected community I was impressed that people were consistently friendly, open and helpful to me. They were notably generous with their time and insights. Somehow the kindness and the care consistently exceeded my expectations. I finally concluded that there is a level of emotional intelligence across the community that is consistently high. And with their emotional intelligence and self-awareness people are happy and quite pleasant to be with. This in turn helps with the relationship-intensive nature of the business, and is fed by that as well.

Richard Beckhard of MIT was one of the three founders of the field of organization development. He used to teach his students to *"use yourself as a probe"* to understand organizations. By this he meant,

> *"Notice how you feel, how people are. Compare and contrast your perceptions in this way, and if you experience consistent patterns, consistent differences, explore what they mean."*[4]

For the past few months I have been immersed in the connected community, and I've been using my body as a probe. My overarching impression is one of calm, of a network of people who while they work hard, stay centered. I have come to the conclusion that I can't fairly describe the connected community without at least noting this deeper sense, this feeling. And, consistent with the studies of Christakis and Fowler, this calm seems contagious.

I commented on this one day to Charlene Marini, an ARM executive, former chip designer and soon to be segment head for the Internet-of-things as we sat — calmly — in the ARM offices in San Jose.

Charlene surprised me by saying, *"Of course."*

From Charlene's perspective, the feeling I was sensing is part of being competent in the job. ARM is in the relationship business and it is essential that ARM staff be emotionally intelligent. Emotionally intelligent people don't go about their day all stressed out. People within the company are very intellectual, and it is standard that discussions are solved by logic and facts. ARM intends to be a thoughtful and precise business culture, but it also intends to be an emotionally healthy one.

Charlene spoke of people being "ARM shaped" — a widely used term of art in the company — and tried to describe what that signified. She gave an example of someone who would be unlikely to succeed. She described how some people become manic under stress. ARM people "roll with things."[5]

ARM people work mostly in teams, and accomplishments are celebrated and evaluated as a team. Individuals do not as a rule get kudos.

Charlene mentioned that evaluations at ARM focus on teamwork.

I followed up with Ian Thornton at ARM corporate headquarters, and received the following email:[6]

"Every year, everyone gets measured using the following table:

	Needs Significant Improvement	Needs Improvement	Good	Excellent	Outstanding
Delivery					
Teamwork & Selflessness					
Constructive Proactivity					
Partner and Customer Focus					

Employees mark themselves. Managers mark them too. You then compare notes, and the differences are discussed. The results of those conversations are sent up to the manager's manager. I would expect that most companies have similar devices, but at ARM these are taken very seriously. We use it to reinforce organizational values and culture. Employees who display those values are called "ARM-shaped" (literally, we do) and remember that ARM's logo is a blue square, so there is some British tongue-in-cheek humour in that comment. I am proud to be a blue square."

Early on in this research I found myself realizing with surprise that within the connected community, interviewees were quite comfortable talking about money — about pricing, margins, market sizes, cost structures and so on. It dawned on me that in most business settings money is not talked about openly or comfortably, particularly among people who share the same value chain. Why is this? I think the explanation may be quite simple: In most business ecosystems there is a high degree of secrecy because it is understood that the parties are out for themselves, and winners do not want their returns to be seen while losers do not want to reveal their weakness.

By contrast, in the connected community there is a genuine desire for others to succeed, recognition that any given company depends on the success of the whole, and a willingness therefore to be more open about finances.

Finally, one of the most robust theories in social psychology pertains to "cognitive dissonance."[7] People have great difficulty keeping in awareness two conflicting ideas. One of my first interviewees had read an account of how Goldman Sachs executives called clients "muppets," — not in a good way. He was insulted by the idea, and couldn't reconcile how they could deal with daily duplicity. For him, there would have been too much cognitive dissonance to reconcile cheating a client while having lunch with him and asking about his family. The answer, I believe, is that the executive would "objectify" the client, seeing him as stupid, unworthy or otherwise deserving of poor treatment — and not as "a person like me."

This reminds me of a book I read years ago, on the essence of relationships.

More than 90 years ago (English translation 75 years ago), the noted Jewish philosopher and Rabbi Martin Buber published a small religious book called I and Thou. The book eventually became an unlikely best seller, sold millions of copies and is still taught in colleges today, most often in social psychology or religion courses.[8]

Buber made a simple but powerful distinction. He argued that people have two underlying ways of relating to the world. One of the ways evolved to cope with objects: he called it "I-It" — the world as filled with "its," or objects. This could include objectifying other people and seeing them as blockages, or tools or enemies to dispatch. It often includes treating oneself as an "it" to prod and drive to success without serious regard for personal and community health.

The other way evolved for living in relationship with other people and God, and was based on our innate capacity for empathy. This way of relating needs to be engaged in order to understand where others are coming from, to listen to and respect their points of view, and to signal our goodwill in non-verbal cues as well as words. It also teaches we can respect ourselves as well, and that this care is consistent with long-term productivity and creativity. This mode he called "I-Thou."

For me personally, the most unexpected feature of my experience doing this study is that the leaders I have met are surprisingly — well, what can I say — I-Thou.

The connected community is no utopia, but it is, to my mind, comparatively advanced. I hope that in this chapter and in this book I have at least begun to make the case that the current success of the connected community is due to a system of mutually reinforcing features centered on cooperation and differentiation. If this is correct, then further study should enable us to say more about what is going on here and perhaps even start to imagine what might come next.

NOTES

[1] Connected, Nicholas A. Christakis and James H. Fowler, Little, Brown, 2009
http://www.amazon.com/Connected-Surprising-Power-Social-
Networks/dp/0316036145/ref=reader_auth_dp

[2] Fowler, J. and N. Christakis. 2008. Dynamic spread of happiness in a large social network,
British Medical Journal, 337: a2338; Fowler, J. and N. Christakis. 2010. Cooperative behavior
cascades in social networks. Proceedings of the National Academy of Science, USA, 107:
5334-38

[3] Supercooperators, Martin Nowak, Free Press, 2011

[4] Richard Beckhard, Class Lecture, Organization Development, Massachusetts Institute of
Technology, 1978

[5] Charlene Marini, ARM Holdings, personal communication, March 2013

[6] Ian Thornton, ARM Holdings, personal communication, April 2013

[7] A Theory of Cognitive Dissonance, Leon Festinger, Stanford University Press, 1957

[8] I and Thou, Martin Buber, 1923, English trans. 1937

Acknowledgements

I want to thank those who gave generously of their goodwill, insights, wisdom, data sets, and time: People in the connected community invited me into their fascinating worlds. As other authors have said better than me: the insights are mostly theirs, the mistakes are all mine. If I have missed anyone please let me know. Thanks so very much to:

Paramesh Gopi	AMCC
Charles Huang	Cadence
Pankaj Major	Cadence
Karl Freund	Calxeda
Nicole St. Claire Knobloch	Concord Bookshop
Robert Hormuth	Dell
Matteo Paris	Ember
Frank Frankovsky	Facebook
Mario Centeno	Freescale
Geoff Lees	Freescale
Charles Cella	GTC Law
JD Deng	Harvard
George Grey	Linaro
Darren Jones	Mass Solar
Wally Rhines	Mentor Graphics
Tom Sanfilippo	Microsoft
Phil Carmack	NVIDIA
Jonathan Masters	Redhat
Phil Dworsky	Synopsys
Rich Goldman	Synopsys
Yvette Huygen	Synopsys
Steve Glaser	Xilinx
Dave Tokic	Xilinx
Warren East	ARM
Ian Ferguson	ARM
Kris Flautner	ARM
Charlene Marini	ARM
Simon Segars	ARM
Ellie Springett	ARM
Ian Thornton	ARM
Raymond Deplazes	Racepoint
RJ Bardsley	Racepoint

A very special thanks to Ellie Springett, Charlene Marini and Ian Thornton for conceiving — in classic ARM fashion — of a partner-centered editorially-independent study of the connected community, for providing access to leaders of the company and the community, and for being super effective, fun, insightful, wise and emotionally intelligent, usually all at once. Amazing! Thank you so very much.

We work in communities of thought as well as action. The influence of two streams of thought can be felt in the connected community. Marco Iansiti's writing on business ecosystems is being used in the connected community as a manual for leading business ecosystems. His clarity has been instrumental in helping leaders generalize the concept and apply it to the more than a thousand ecologies of shared purpose within and across the connected community. Clayton Christensen's teaching on disruptive technologies provides inspiration and a fresh template for upsetting establishments and advancing society. It is clear to me that the connected community itself, with its open ecosystems and open-source communities is itself a disruptive technology.

About the Author

James F. Moore is a former Berkman Fellow at Harvard's Berkman Center for Internet & Society, and an authority on leadership and change in large-scale systems. His work combines organizational, economic and technology studies.

Moore originated the concept of business ecosystems in articles in Upside Magazine and the Harvard Business Review. His May/June 1993 HBR article, "Predators & Prey: A new ecology of competition," won the year's McKinsey Award. It was published 20 years ago this month.

During the 1990s Moore chose to study and advise very large-scale networks of organizations—those he terms "first generation business ecosystems." In the 2000s he chose to work with Internet-enabled communities including those in science and academics, politics, community organizing and open source software—what he calls "second generation ecosystems." Presently Moore is studying a new "third generation" model that combines the benefits of both predecessors. This model seems to be most advanced in the population described in this book, a population of more than a thousand interacting business ecosystems, collectively radiating from the semiconductor sector into the many other economic sectors it influences.

Moore has chosen to conduct research or teach at the Harvard Business School, the Stanford Program on Organizations, the Darden Business School at the University of Virginia, as well as at the Berkman Center. His work has been published widely including best-selling *The Death of Competition: Leadership and Strategy in the Age of Business Ecosystems* (Harper Business, 1996).

6049003R00051

Printed in Great Britain
by Amazon.co.uk, Ltd.,
Marston Gate.